CLEOPATRA

CLEOPATRA

FACT AND FICTION

BARBARA WATTERSON

AMBERLEY

For my granddaughters, Alice and Lily

First published 2017

Amberley Publishing
The Hill, Stroud
Gloucestershire, GL5 4EP

www.amberley-books.com

Copyright © Barbara Watterson, 2017

The right of Barbara Watterson to be identified
as the Author of this work has been asserted
in accordance with the Copyrights, Designs
and Patents Act 1988.

ISBN 978 1 4456 6965 6 (hardback)
ISBN 978 1 4456 6966 3 (ebook)

British Library Cataloguing in Publication Data.
A catalogue record for this book is available
from the British Library.

Typesetting and Origination by Amberley Publishing
Printed in the UK.

CONTENTS

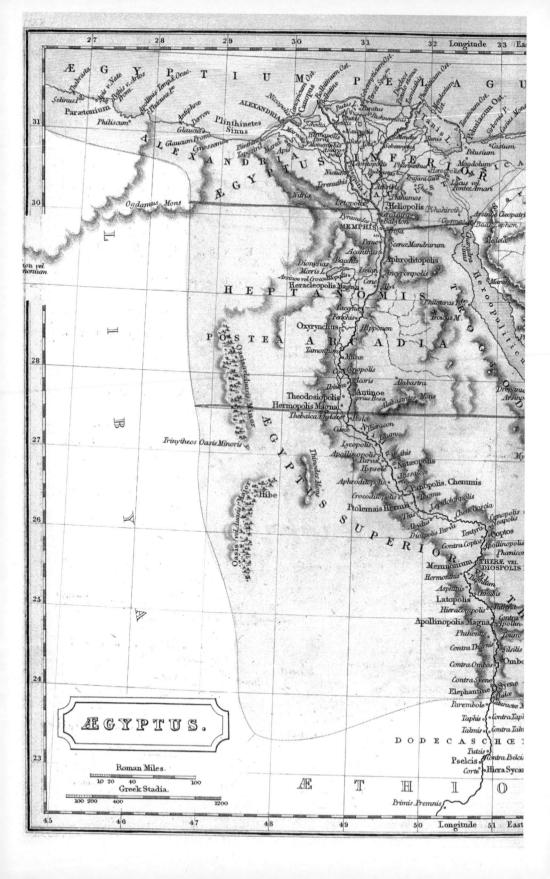

ÆGYPTUS.

Roman Miles.
10 20   40   100

Greek Stadia.
100 200   400   1200

East from 34 Greenwich 35 36 37 38 39 40

Alata

Bethel
Philadelphia
Ekron
Azotus JERUSALEM Hesbon
(Ascalon) Nebo
(Gaza) Eglon Hebron Callirhoe
(Gezar) (Beersheba) Masada L. Asphaltites
Rhinocorura Thamara Areopolis vel Moab)
(Her Moab)

Elusa Hagrad 31
Eboda Tophel
Bozamma Thoada Bozra Oboda
Hadeh Harnea Carcar Arindela
Hor M. (Petra) Phainon
Gubba Gypsaria Maon
Paran vel Faran Haura Zaimona 30

ARABIA

Chaulotæi
Agubeni

DESERTA

Kedar vel Cedrei

Thaditæ

ARABES SCENITÆ

Ancale
Segir Madiana

Sideni
Saraceni
Gæa
Modiana Laba Thema
Jovis I.
Thamedite Apatei vel
Nabatæi

Negra

Hippus Mons
Aneud Hippus
Mochura Iathrippa
Leucecome v.Lathrippa
Raunathi Vicus Alvare
Timagenis I. Batnizomenes
Thamudeni
Raunathi Vicus
Chersonesi P. Iambia
Charmuthas

Cinædocolpitæ
Copar
Agathanis I. Dæmonum I.

Zaaram
Arga

S. Hall. Del. et Sculp.

East from 52 Ferro 53 54 55 56 57

CHAPTER ONE

PERCEPTIONS OF CLEOPATRA

Cleopatra is one of the greatest romantic figures in history, the queen of Egypt whose beauty and allure is legendary. We think we know her story, but our knowledge of this is largely gleaned from Shakespeare's *Antony and Cleopatra*. Shakespeare was inspired by Thomas North's 1579 translation of Plutarch's *Lives of the Noble Greeks and Romans*. Plutarch, however, was only sixteen years old when Cleopatra died and he seems to have obtained much of his information about her from a diary kept by her personal physician, Olympus.

In the middle of the first century BC, Cleopatra caught the attention of Rome by captivating the two most powerful Romans of the day, Julius Caesar and Mark Antony. She outlived both and attempted to suborn a third, her mortal enemy, Octavius Caesar, the first of the Roman Emperors. Having failed to do so she destroyed herself: but her hostility towards Octavius lived on in the memories of his successors. Their supporters heaped opprobrium upon her and there were few unbiased accounts of the woman who exerted what the Romans thought of as a malign influence on her two Roman lovers and threatened the safety of Rome itself.

Cleopatra was highly intelligent and politically astute. She also wielded great power. Even today many men are uncomfortable with powerful women and denigrate them as unfeminine, though given that Cleopatra's Roman detractors claimed that she used her feminine wiles to entrap Caesar and Antony they could hardly accuse her of being masculine.

Even Zenobia, queen of the Syrian city of Palmyra in the third-century AD, did not attract the criticism directed at Cleopatra, in spite of the fact that she had the temerity to capture Egypt, a Roman province, consolidating her position there by claiming that she was a descendant of Cleopatra and then turning her attention to Anatolia, conquering Roman territory as far west as Ancyra (modern Ankara). Subsequently, she conquered Syria, Palestine and Lebanon using military might combined with propaganda. In AD 272 she was defeated at Homs in Syria by the Emperor Aurelian and taken in chains, reputedly made of gold, to Rome. She was no longer a threat and largely disappeared from history.

Cleopatra's detractors were writing years after her death and most had never even seen her, let alone been introduced to her. One who met her several times in Rome was Marcus Tullius Cicero (106-43 BC), the great orator, writer and statesman, who found her to be an 'uncommonly impertinent' harlot. In a letter to his friend, Atticus, Cicero wrote that he detested the queen and could not bear to think of her insolence when she was living in Julius Caesar's villa.

How Cleopatra displayed this insolence and whether it was exhibited to Cicero himself or to others he does not say. If the Queen was indeed insolent, it was perhaps a defence mechanism on Cleopatra's part against Roman nobles who made clear their disapproval not only of a woman wielding great power but also of one who, by living with Caesar, flouted the social mores of the day.

Pliny the Elder (*c*. AD23-79), the Roman historian and scientist, accused Cleopatra of unseemly opulence and extravagance, citing as an example of the latter the wager she had with Mark Antony that she could spend ten million sesterces, worth about 1746 pounds of gold, on a single banquet. The meal served was ordinary enough but after the last course Cleopatra took one of the pair of pearl earrings that she was wearing - the two pearls, according to Pliny, that were the largest ever found - and dropped the priceless jewel, said to have been worth ten million sesterces by itself, into a chalice containing wine vinegar. Pearls, being mostly calcium carbonate, can be dissolved in wine vinegar providing the acetic acid is strong enough. Cleopatra toasted Antony and then drank her pearl 'magistery', or essence, which was thought to be an aphrodisiac, presumably because of an association between pearls and Venus, the goddess of love, both being from the sea. Cleopatra was about to dissolve the second pearl but was prevented from doing so by Lucius Munatius Plancus, a Roman senator who had been asked to judge the wager. This pearl was eventually given to the Temple of Venus Genetrix in Rome where it adorned the statue of the goddess.

Flavius Josephus (AD 37-*c*.100), the Jewish historian who gained Roman citizenship and settled in Rome, was no admirer of Cleopatra. He claimed that she was a slave to her lusts and would stop at no wickedness, even violating the tombs of her ancestors. He claimed that her greed drove her to order the temples of Egypt to be ransacked in order to obtain gold and other precious commodities. There is no evidence for this; and in any case, Cleopatra, like all rulers of Egypt, was considered to be the high priest of every temple and therefore entitled to dispose of its property. It may be that she ordered her agents to obtain from temples the wherewithal to fund her war against Rome; but that was, after all, in defence of Egypt. Josephus also claimed that Cleopatra attempted to seduce King Herod, a story that was never related by anyone else and may just be an example of Josephus' extreme aversion to the Egyptian queen.

The poet Lucan (AD 39-65), author of the epic poem *Pharsalia,* a history of the civil wars between Julius Caesar and Pompey, described Cleopatra as 'the shame of Egypt, the lascivious fury who became the bane of Rome'; and another poet, Horace (65-8 BC), described her as a mad queen who plotted to demolish the Capitol and topple the Empire.

Dio Cassius (AD 150-235), the Roman historian, thought of her as a woman of insatiable avarice and unbounded passion. He claimed that she was a ruthless manipulator willing to sacrifice Mark Antony in favour of an alliance with Octavius Caesar, confident that she could seduce her enemy because of her conviction that she was entitled to the love of all men.

Cleopatra's Appearance

Cleopatra was descended from a long line of Macedonian Greek kings who formed the dynasty[1] named after its founder, Ptolemy Lagides (see page 23), who had been one of Alexander's generals. No reliably authenticated portrait busts of her have yet been discovered, although there are several coins with the queen's head stamped on them. On the coins, she is depicted wearing her hair in a bun at the nape of her neck and the royal diadem, a wide band made of silver, encircles her head. Both the bun and the diadem are in the Greek style rather than the Egyptian. Her eyes are large and her lips finely chiselled but her nose is hooked and her jowls somewhat heavy. Cleopatra is shown in reliefs on the walls of several Egyptian temples of the Ptolemaic period, notably that of the goddess Hathor at Denderah, but these are conventional representations rather than actual portraits. The Denderah reliefs show the queen in typical Ptolemaic style, with a chubby-cheeked face and an incipient double chin.

We can only speculate about what the colour of Cleopatra's hair, skin and eyes was. Since her ancestry was Macedonian Greek, her hair was probably dark brown but could have been fair; her eyes were probably dark brown but may have been blue, hazel or grey; and her skin probably had an olive hue. She seems to have been not much more than five feet tall with fine bones and a slim, graceful figure. No doubt her appearance was enhanced by the cosmetics that the Egyptians had for centuries been skilled at applying; and by the unguents and perfumes that, Pliny observed, turned the heads of everyone when an Egyptian woman passed by.

Cleopatra's perceived beauty seems not to have manifested itself in her face. Plutarch observed that her actual beauty was apparently not in itself so remarkable that none could be compared with her. It was the impact of her presence that was irresistible and it was the charm of her conversation and the character that marked all that she said or did that was bewitching. Above all, it was the sound of her voice, which, he said, was like an instrument of many strings. She could pass from one language to another, so that there were few of the barbarian nations that she had to speak to through an interpreter; to most of them she spoke herself in their own tongue. She had learned not only Egyptian but also the languages of the Ethiopians, Hebrews, Arabians, Syrians, Medes, Parthians, and many others, even including the Troglodytes, an ancient group of cave-dwelling people from the African Red Sea coast. Cleopatra's willingness to learn so many languages is all the more surprising since most of the kings of the Ptolemaic dynasty, her predecessors, had not troubled themselves even to learn Egyptian, the language spoken by their subjects. Dio Cassius also remarked upon Cleopatra's voice, calling it 'most charming'; and claimed that she knew how to make herself agreeable to everyone. Neither he nor Plutarch, however, had ever heard Cleopatra speak. It appears from literary compositions that the Egyptians considered that the tone of a woman's voice should be sweet - but she should not speak too much! Plutarch and Dio Cassius would recognise Cleopatra in these definitions; and no doubt both would agree that a woman should strive to be seen and not heard.

The Egyptians appreciated beauty in a woman and had their own opinions on what was the ideal: she should be slender and graceful with a slim waist and small, firm breasts; her neck should be long, her eyes clear, her skin pale and untouched by the sun, and her hair blue-black.[2] There are many examples of beautiful women in reliefs and paintings in ancient Egyptian tombs, none of them portraits but idealised representations conforming to this norm. The most famous image of beauty is perhaps the life-size bust of Nefertiti, now in the Neues Museum in Berlin, which was sculpted around 1345 BC. It is made of limestone overlaid with coloured plaster; and its authenticity as a portrait of the queen is confirmed by other representations such as the unpainted yellow quartzite bust now in Berlin and another quartzite head now in the Egyptian Museum in Cairo. Such busts were never meant to be seen by the majority of Egyptians and in any case these three lay undiscovered in their sculptor's workshop for centuries until modern archaeological excavations in the late nineteenth and early twentieth centuries uncovered them. They all show Nefertiti with high cheekbones, a full-lipped, sensuous mouth, almond-shaped eyes, a small, straight nose and a long, slim neck. On the Berlin painted bust, her skin is a smooth, creamy colour; but she is wearing her distinctive all-covering headdress so the colour of her hair cannot be ascertained.

It would be safe to say that Cleopatra did not conform to the Egyptian ideals of physical beauty. It would also be safe to say that none of the many actresses to have played her on stage and screen look anything like her (see Chapter 6).

CHAPTER TWO

THE PTOLEMIES

Alexander III, king of the northern Greek kingdom of Macedon, known today as Alexander the Great, arrived in Egypt in October 332 BC, changing the course of Egyptian history. Without Alexander, the country would probably have remained a subjugated part of the Persian Empire, Cleopatra might still have come into existence some two and a half centuries later, but she would never have been Queen of Egypt.

Alexander was born in 356 BC, the son of Philip II, king of Macedon, and Olympias, princess of Epirus (modern Albania). Philip had become king three years earlier, at the age of twenty-three. A great and successful general, his ambition was to unite the city-states of Greece under his leadership; but it took him over twenty years to achieve his aim, and then only after he had defeated the Athenians at the Battle of Chaeronea in 338 BC. He became Supreme Commander of the united armies of Greece, ready to lead them into battle against their greatest rival, Persia. Two years after Chaeronea, Darius III became King of Persia.

In that same year, Philip of Macedon arranged a marriage between his daughter, Cleopatra, and her uncle, Alexander, king of Epirus. The marriage celebrations, which Olympias, the mother of the bride, did not attend because of her estrangement from her husband, were held at Aigai in the oldest of the Macedonian palaces and went on for several days. On the last day, Philip took part in a procession to the theatre. He insisted on going without bodyguards, instead being escorted only by his son, Alexander, and his new son-in-law, Alexander of Epirus. At the entrance to the theatre, a young soldier, Pausanias, lay in wait and as Philip passed by sprang out and stabbed him to death. Pausanias was killed by other soldiers before he could be questioned about whether he had acted alone or been part of a plot. Suspicion fell on Olympias, who nevertheless hurried to Aigai to ensure that her son succeded to the throne; and when she got there had the body of her husband's assassin taken down from the stake to which it had been tied, and had it burned honourably on a funeral pyre built over Philip's own.

Philip of Macedon had at least seven wives, of whom Olympias, a forceful, ruthless woman, not known to hesitate over having perceived rivals killed, was the most powerful. She claimed that she was descended from Achilles, the great Greek hero of the Trojan War, and that the blood of Helen of Troy ran in her veins. Since Helen's father was said to have been Zeus, King of the Gods, who, disguised as a swan, had seduced her human mother, Leda, Olympias was claiming divine descent. She probably married Philip in 357

BC and less than a year later, Alexander was born. Olympias unashamedly hinted that the baby's father was not the King of Macedon but Zeus, King of the Gods. How this was achieved Olympias never explained, but she claimed that Zeus ordered his daughter, Artemis, goddess of, amongst other things, childbirth, to leave her temple at Ephesus to attend his son's birth. Curiously, it was while Artemis was absent from her sanctuary that her temple was set alight by Herostratus, a wanton act of vandalism that he carried out because he wanted to be famous.

At the age of twenty, Alexander had inherited not only the throne of Macedon that, thanks to his father, was rich and flourishing, but also the leadership of the Greek city-states. In the early spring of 334 BC, Alexander crossed the Hellespont, known today as the Dardanelles, into Anatolia (modern Turkey) at the head of an army of some 35,000 men. In May of that year, he met the Persian army led by Darius at Granicus, a river east of Troy: the Persians were defeated and Darius fled the field of battle. Six months later, in November 333 BC, the armies met again, this time at Issus, near to the present-day town of Iskenderun. Again the Persians were defeated: Darius fled and his wife and children were captured. Alexander's third and final battle against Darius took place in July, 331 BC, at Gaugamela, east of the Tigris river in Mesopotamia. Alexander was victorious once again and Darius took refuge in Bactria (Afghanistan), where several months later he was murdered. Alexander went on to capture Persia itself.

After the Battle of Issus, the logical step would have been to proceed straight away to Mesopotamia. Alexander chose to divert part of his army to Egypt, the capture of which was not necessary to his overall plan since it lay on the periphery of the Persian Empire. The reason for him doing so can only be guessed at but it is more than possible that he wished to consult the famous Oracle at the temple of Zeus Ammon in the Siwa Oasis in the Western Desert. Zeus, after all, was his divine father, at least according to Olympias. On 14 November 332 BC, Alexander allowed himself to be crowned King of Egypt by the priests of Memphis, thus, according to Egyptian tradition, becoming a god. In January of the following year, he chose a site on the Mediterranean coast some 178 km (111 miles) west of Memphis, to be the first, and greatest, of the many cities than were to be named Alexandria in his honour. He is said to have marked out its ground plan himself, although the official foundation of the city was set at 7 April, 331 BC. Alexander had selected an excellent site for his new city: it was on the coast where the cool prevailing offshore winds ensured a healthy climate, it had a deep, sheltered harbour and only two narrow land approaches, both of which could easily be defended.

According to Alexander's second-century AD biographer, Arrian, the king was then seized with a longing to visit Ammon in Siwa, and set out on a three-week-long trek over 500 km (300 miles) of desert to the oasis. There, he consulted the Oracle, although what it said to him he did not divulge except to say that it had told him what he wanted to know. From an Egyptian point of view, it was appropriate that Alexander should seek recognition as the son of the State God, Amun, whom the Greeks knew as Ammon: theogany, that is, the practice of a god begetting a child with the wife of an earthly king, being a long-accepted way of a king validating his claim to the Egyptian throne. From Alexander's point of view, Amun's recognition of him as his son assuaged any doubts he may have had that Philip was indeed his father, for in the tradition of theogany there is no suggestion that the earthly father had been cuckolded by the god.

Eight years after consulting the Oracle at Siwa, that is, on 13 June, 323 BC, Alexander lay dead in Babylon. His empire was divided among his generals who, out of respect to their great leader, ruled its different countries as satraps, or governors, during the reigns of Alexander's successors. When the last heir, Alexander's son born after his death, was murdered in 304 BC, they lost no time in declaring themselves kings of their respective satrapies. At Alexander's death, Ptolemy Lagides (son of Lagus) had been allowed to claim Egypt, a country so far from Macedon that it was the least-regarded satrapy of all, in spite of its great wealth. Ptolemy appreciated the wealth but perhaps above all he valued Egypt's position: on the edge of Alexander's empire and therefore not in direct contact with the other satrapies. Ptolemy need not have been too prescient to realise that it would not be long before the ambitious rulers of the new kingdoms would go to war with each other.

Ptolemy, whose name means 'warlike', was born in 366 BC, the son of Lagus, an obscure country squire in Macedon, and Arsinoe, a princess of the royal family. The fact that Lagus was allowed to marry a woman so far above his station gave rise to the suspicion that Lagus had been persuaded to marry her because she was pregnant with the child of King Philip. Whatever the true origins of Ptolemy's paternity, Philip always took a great interest in him and made him one of the seven boys of good family who were chosen to be Alexander's companions. When King Alexander left Macedon on what he termed his 'great adventure', Ptolemy went with him and in the military campaigns that followed distinguished himself so much that he was made a member of the royal bodyguard.

The Egyptians had welcomed Alexander not as a conqueror but as a liberator who freed them from the onerous rule of the detested Persians, a ruler who treated them and their customs with respect. The shrewd Ptolemy must have calculated that Alexander's actions had made Egypt a country that was easier to govern than some, especially by Ptolemy himself, who had rid the Egyptians of a tyrannous satrap, thus making him popular with the populace. It is very likely that Ptolemy, like Alexander before him, had familiarised himself with the customs of the country and was aware of the belief that when the god-king of Egypt, Osiris, died, his son, Horus, became responsible for his burial in order to claim the throne. Thus every living king was regarded as a Horus and every deceased king as an Osiris; and when a king died, his successor, not in every instance his son, acted as Horus and by burying his predecessor established his right to the throne.

Unlike Alexander, Ptolemy was not a king. He could not, therefore, claim to be the son of Amun. He had, however, laid claim to Alexander's body and brought it back from Babylon to Egypt, where it lay at rest in Memphis until a suitably magnificent tomb could be built for it in Alexandria. The traditional burial place for Macedonian kings was at Aigai (Vergina), the ancient capital of Macedon, but perhaps the other generals in Alexander's army had deemed it fitting that he should be buried in his great new city. This was not what Alexander had wanted: he had asked that his body be thrown into the river Euphrates and so disappear, leaving behind the impression that he had been spirited away to take his place alongside his heavenly father, Zeus-Ammon. If his followers could not bring themselves to dispose of his body in that way then he asked that it should be taken to Siwa and buried in the temple there. According to the historian and geographer, Strabo[1] who visited Alexandria sometime between 30 and 25 BC, the tomb of Alexander was located in the royal palace area known as the Sema (the 'body'). Ptolemy had a coffin of hammered gold made for Alexander, but in about 90 BC, the golden coffin was plundered and replaced by a new coffin made of glass or crystal. When Octavian visited Alexander's tomb nearly three hundred years after the burial, he is said to have placed a golden diadem upon the head of the mummified Alexander, and flowers at the tomb.[2]

By burying Alexander, Ptolemy laid claim, according to Egyptian tradition, to the throne of Egypt. The tradition was based upon the story of the god, Osiris, who became king of Egypt and whose burial was carried out by his son, Horus. Since every king of Egypt was deemed to be the earthly representation of Horus, and every dead king the embodiment of the dead Osiris, the man who buried a deceased king was acting as Horus to that king's Osiris and thereby was entitled to rule Egypt. Ptolemy did not immediately proclaim himself king but waited until 304 BC when the last of Alexander's heirs died. He then became, at the age of sixty-three, the first king of the Ptolemaic dynasty, the last dynasty of kings to rule ancient Egypt. Ptolemy, Macedonian Greek, might have been expected to act according to the norms of his own culture rather than to those of pharaonic Egypt which were somewhat different. From the outset, however, he took pains to integrate with his new domain, building temples dedicated to Egyptian deities and making full use of the administrative talents of the priesthood. He styled himself Ptolemy Soter (Saviour) and adopted the royal titulary that had been used by the pharaohs.[3] As king his name was engraved on public monuments enclosed in a cartouche, the oblong shape inside which Egyptian royal names were traditionally inscribed, as 'Ptulmis, beloved of Amun, Son of the Sun (Re)'. Ptolemy I Soter ruled Egypt for the next twenty years; his dynasty was to rule Egypt for nearly three centuries.

Ptolemy I Soter's immediate concern was the territorial ambitions of his erstwhile companions-in-arms. In order to thwart them, he built up a buffer state between his territory and theirs by acquiring extensive tracts of land in the Aegean and western Asia, including Palestine, Coelesyria, the fertile valley between Phoenicia and the Syrian desert, and Cyprus.

Under Ptolemy I Soter, the main lines of the Ptolemaic legal, administrative and military systems were put into place. He allowed the ancient deities of Egypt to be worshipped and encouraged their temples to flourish. Ptolemy I Soter introduced a new deity into Egypt, a hybrid god called Serapis, whose name was a combination of two ancient Egyptian deities, Osiris, god of the dead, and Apis, the sacred bull of Memphis, but whose chief attributes were Hellenistic, being those of Zeus, Dionysos, the god of fertility and wine, and Asklepios, the god of medicine. Serapis was thus a god of the underworld and of fertility, a physician and helper of mankind. A great temple was built for him in Alexandria, the Serapeum. Ptolemy I Soter intended his new god to appeal to both Greeks and Egyptians but he was never fully accepted by the Egyptians.

Soon after Ptolemy became satrap of Egypt he paid a visit to the site of Alexandria to see how work on Alexander's new city was progressing. It had been ten years or so since the great town planner, Deinocrates of Chalcedon, known for his work on the city of Ephesus, had been entrusted with drawing up a plan of the city according to Alexander's own dictates. He and his architect, Sostratus of Cnidus, had made great progress. The city, designed on an axial grid system, had two main avenues, each 30 metres wide, running from east to west and north to south. They were intersected at right angles by numerous smaller streets. The island of Pharos, which lay off the north coast, was linked to the mainland by a breakwater, or mole, called the Heptastadium, on either side of which was a harbour, the Great Port to the east and Eunostos to the west. Alexandria had two districts: Rhakotis in the the west, on the shores of Lake Mareotis, the people's district built over the ancient village of Raqote that had stood on the site; and Brucheion, the royal palace area. In due course, over a quarter of Alexandria was covered with palaces, temples, the most famous of which was the Serapeum (see above), and public buildings, including baths, gymnasia, a hippodrome and a theatre. They were built of stone and their architecture was Greek. The city was eventually inhabited by some 300,000 free citizens and at least that number of slaves. Its chief industries were linen weaving, glass making and papyrus manufacture. Although Alexander had intended that Alexandria should be a great cosmopolis in which Macedonians, Greeks, Jews and Egyptians should all live together amicably, Deinocrates had designed separate areas for Jews and Egyptians. There is no suggestion that these areas were in any sense ghettoes in which non-Greeks were forced to live, but it is a fact that Jews largely kept to their own quarter in the east of the city, and Egyptians to theirs in Rhakotis. Egyptians were later to form a second native quarter on the island of Pharos.

Ptolemy I Soter realised that Alexandria had to be treated differently from the rest of the country: the city was said to 'adjoin' Egypt, and it was always considered to be in but not of the country. Alexander had intended it to be an Hellenistic city run on democratic lines, with every male Greek or Macedonian inhabitant being a citizen with a citizen's right to carry arms and to enjoy the freedom to meet in open assembly to discuss political grievances. Jews, Egyptians and women had no such rights. Ptolemy I Soter was well aware of the danger of Alexandria becoming a city state and so, although he allowed its citizens to carry arms, they were not permitted to use them; and although they could discuss political grievances they were not granted the political power that would have enabled them to redress them. This does not seem to have worried Alexandria's citizens unduly, and they were content to leave government to the king.

Under Ptolemy I Soter, Alexandria became not only a great centre of trade and commerce but was also well on the way to being the supreme centre of scholarship in the ancient world. Ptolemy I Soter sought advice from Demetrius of

Phalerum, the great orator and philosopher, on how best to attract scholars to Alexandria. Demetrius recommended that an academy of the arts and sciences should be built where scholars could meet and study: thus the Mouseion of Alexandria came into being, named after the Nine Muses, the Greek goddesses who, according to mythology, presided over the arts and sciences and inspired those who studied them. It was an imposing edifice built near the royal palace; and was soon accompanied by a great library. Ptolemy I Soter's careful stewardship of Egypt had made the country wealthy and he was well able to invite men of learning to Alexandria where, if they wished, they could stay, living at state expense. In the Mouseion, scholars lived, ate, and walked together, able to enjoy their discussions and work and teach, free from financial burdens. Among the many scholars to enjoy Ptolemy I Soter's hospitality were the mathematician Euclid, the physicians Herophilus and Eristratus, the historian Hecataeus and the grammarian Zenodotus. There is no record of an Egyptian being invited to enjoy what the Mouseion had to offer: the Greeks were not interested in Egyptian culture, only in the produce and taxes that the rest of Egypt supplied to Alexandria.

Under the Ptolemies, Alexandria was to become the intellectual capital of the western world and a great commercial centre. By the middle of the first century BC, it had a population of about half a million free citizens and was immensely prosperous. Large merchant fleets were despatched to Ethiopia and India through the canal that linked the Nile with the Red Sea that had been started in the reign of Necho II (610-595 BC) and brought into use again under Ptolemy II Philadelphus (see below); and to the rest of the world from the great harbours on the Mediterranean.

Alexandria was a strange city, without any of the normal democratic institutions enjoyed by even the smallest Greek city. Officials were appointed by the king, who announced his decisions by decree. The only way Alexandrians could make their opinion known was by rioting, which they did frequently, earning them a reputation for turbulence. There were several major revolts in Alexandria, first under the Ptolemies and then under the Romans: in the reigns of several Roman emperors, Alexandria suffered a series of massacres and gradually became depopulated.

Ptolemy I Soter abdicated in 285 BC in favour of his son, Ptolemy II Philadelphus ('Beloved of his Brother', 282-246 BC). A year later, at the age of eighty-four, he died. He was the only one of Alexander's royal bodyguards to die of old age, peacefully, in his own bed. The tomb that had been prepared for Alexander's body was finished but empty, the king's body still lying in Memphis. At the insistence of Macedonian veterans, Alexander and Ptolemy I Soter were buried side by side in the Sema, reunited in death.

Under Philadelphus, the Great Library in the Brucheion quarter was developed; and another library, known as the Daughter Library, was built in the Rhakotis quarter in the precincts of the Temple of Serapis, the Serapeum, that had been built for Ptolemy I Soter. Demetrius of Phalerum was commissioned to obtain book-rolls for the library: it is said that he amassed over 50,000 rolls, most of which lay in storage for several years, unexamined and unclassified, until Zenodotus and the poet Callimachus of Cyrene were invited to examine and catalogue them so that they might be available to anyone who wished to consult them. Philadelphus was always in the market for book-rolls and spent unstintingly on them. His son was to be ruthless in obtaining books for the library, at one point refusing to send grain to Athens during a famine unless the city agreed to send a guarantee of repayment in the form of the original copies of the works of the playwrights Sophocles, Aeschylus and Euripides. Once in Alexandria, the originals were carefully copied and the copies sent back to Athens. The originals were placed in the Great Library.

Philadelphus ordered the construction of a great lighthouse in Alexandria, to be built on the eastern tip of the island of Pharos. It was the island that gave its name to the lighthouse that was to become one of the Seven Wonders of the Ancient World. Built in marble according to the design of Sostratus of Cnidus (see page 27), it had five levels and was probably about 140 metres (455 feet) high. The first three floors were square, the fourth octagonal and the fifth circular, with the area of each of the levels smaller than the one below. The lighthouse was topped with a roof equipped with metal mirrors that gleamed in the sun, enabling the lighthouse to be seen from a distance and reflecting ships too far away to be observed from ground level. At night, a beacon was burned as a guide to navigators. He continued to welcome scholars to the Mouseion, notably Eratosthenes, the geographer who in 240 BC measured the diameter of the earth correctly to within 87 km (54 miles).

Philadelphus' first queen was Arsinoe, the daughter of Lysimachus of Thrace, who was himself married to

Philadelphus' sister, also named Arsinoe. In 281 BC, Lysimachus and Seleucus of Babylon, the last of Alexander's satraps, finally managed to kill each other, and the widowed Arsinoe returned to Alexandria. In less than two years, she had engineered her sister-in-law's exile to Coptos in southern Egypt, accused of plotting her brother's murder. Princess Arsinoe then married Philadelphus, like her a child of Ptolemy I Soter's wife, Berenice, the first of that name, making this a marriage between full-blood siblings. Brother-sister marriages were not uncommon in Egypt but foreign, not to say anathema, to Greeks. The name Philadelphus was adapted, rather pointedly, when the pair were deified as Theoi Philadelphoi, that is, 'sibling-loving gods'. The union was not met with universal acclaim by Greeks, but Philadelphus and Arsinoe II seem to have tried to convince them of the propriety of their incestuous marriage by drawing attention, thanks to a poem written by Theocritus, then resident in Alexandria, to the union of Zeus and Hera, siblings, although in this case, divine siblings. They also drew attention to the Egyptian god, Osiris, who married his sister, Isis. Thus Philadelphus and Arsinoe II established the practice of brother-sister marriage, the first but not the last of the dynasty to indulge in it. The Ptolemies took to brother-sister marriages wholeheartedly, with four of them marrying their sisters, one marrying two of his sisters, and another marrying the daughter of his father's mistress. One broke ranks and married his stepmother. The marriage between Philadelphus and Arsinoe II, which lasted for less than ten years until her death in 269 BC, was to be childless, indicating, perhaps, that it was in name only, undertaken for political reasons.

It brought to Philadelphus most of Lysimachus' possessions in the Aegean. Arsinoe II was a woman of great ambition and ability who exerted a decisive influence on Egyptian politics: she set the pattern for later queens in the dynasty to follow.

Ptolemy II Philadelphus was succeeded by Ptolemy III Euergetes I ('The Benefactor', 246-222 BC), the son of his father's first wife, Arsinoe I. He was married to Berenice, the daughter of Magas, stepbrother of Philadelphus and ruler of Cyrenaica, and his wife, Apame, daughter of Antiochus of Syria. On the death of Magas, Cyrenaica was taken back into Egypt's possession. Euergetes I was a highly successful general who enlarged his foreign possessions, with Libya, Nubia, Palestine, Phoenicia, the Cyclades, Cyprus and large parts of south-western Asia falling under Egyptian control. Euergetes I, like his father and grandfather, initiated many reforms and achieved great success in domestic and foreign affairs: but after his death the country was progressively weakened and impoverished by incessant civil war and corruption within the royal family.

Euergetes I realised that a secure and well administered base outwith the confines of Alexandria was necessary for the successful prosecution of his foreign wars, and that the way to achieve this was to persuade the inhabitants of the country at large to cooperate. He, like his Greek subjects, remained resolutely Greek in outlook, culture and language. Egyptians were despised and were particularly scorned for what the Greeks considered to be their peculiar customs. They even mocked the Egyptian gods, although Greeks were normally tolerant of other people's religions. To ensure the efficient running of the country, Euergetes I sought the cooperation of the powerful Egyptian priesthood, in return for which he began commissioning the building of new temples. Temples played a vital role in Egyptian life, though not as places of worship, for only priests and certain privileged people were allowed to enter what was deemed to be the private house of a deity. Temples were great bureaucratic centres, they owned land which they rented out to tenant farmers, their priests ran schools in which children, normally boys, were educated, and in which scribes, doctors and artists were trained. Physician-priests were based within temple precincts, from which they visited the sick or, in some temples, brought patients in to be treated in rudimentary hospitals. Temple scribes drew up all kinds of documents, from records of births and deaths to marriage contracts and law suits, which were kept in the temple archives.

In 237 BC, Euergetes I founded a temple, dedicated to the god, Horus, at Edfu, on the west bank of the Nile some 100 km (60 miles) south of Luxor. Work on the nucleus of the building was begun in 237 BC and completed twenty-five years later in the reign of Euergetes I's son, Ptolemy IV Philopator ('Father-loving', 221-205 BC) (see below). Philopator ordered a chapel dedicated to Imhotep, the ancient Egyptian sage and physician whom the Greeks identified with Asclepius, their god of medicine, to be built on Philae, an island upriver of Egypt's southern border, where Nectanebo I (380-362 BC) had initiated the building of a temple dedicated to the goddess Isis. Later Ptolemies added shrines, chapels and monumental gateways to the Temple of Isis, which became an important religious site for succeeding generations. One of the largest and most impressive temples built in the Ptolemaic era is the Temple of Hathor at Denderah, some sixty-two km (37 miles) north of Luxor, begun in the reign of Ptolemy IX Soter II (116-107 BC) and known today for its reliefs depicting Cleopatra VII and her son by Julius Caesar, Caesarion.

Ptolemy IV Philopator inherited a prosperous Egypt, but unlike the first three Ptolemies, his great-grandfather, grandfather and father before him, he chose to lead a dissolute life of luxury and debauchery. His chief minister was one Sosibius: nothing is known about his ancestry, although judging by his name he was Greek, and nothing is known about his career until he appears at the beginning of Philopator's reign, wielding great influence over the king and seemingly in charge of affairs of state. Within a year of coming to the throne, possibly at the instigation of Sosibius, Philopator had his mother, Berenice, poisoned and his brother, Magas, scalded to death. Sosibius allowed both the finances of Egypt and its military defences to fall into disrepair so that when Antiochus III of Syria declared war against Ptolemy, and invaded Coele-Syria, Egypt was unprepared for battle.

In 217 BC, Antiochus III led an army of some 60,000 soldiers, supported by 6,000 cavalry and 102 Indian elephants, towards Egypt with the intention of conquering the country. On 22 June of that year, Philopator, who had been persuaded to take to the battlefield himself with an army of 5,000 cavalry, 73 African elephants and 70,000 infantry - which, for the first time, contained Egyptians trained to fight in the Macedonian way - met the Syrians at Raphia (modern Rafah, near Gaza). Antiochus III was decisively defeated. It was Agathocles, the brother of the king's mistress, Agathoclia, who had been responsible for a policy of recruiting native Egyptians into the Ptolemaic army; thanks to that policy, the Battle of Raphia, prompted by the conviction of the Egyptian soldiers that the victory was largely due to their efforts, was a great stimulus to Egyptian nationalism. The soldiers rapidly came to resent the fact that they were not given their due recognition, and this resentment, combined with harsh taxation, led to a series of native revolts which, over the next century, caused Egypt to be in a state of frequent insurrection.

In the same year as the Battle of Raphia, Philopator married his sister, Arsinoe, who took seven years before producing an heir. When Philopator died five years later, Arsinoe was quickly disposed of by Sosibius and Agathocles who then appointed themselves guardians of the young king, Ptolemy V Epiphanes ('Made Manifest', 205-180 BC). It took the capable and popular general Tlepolemus, who was in charge of Egypt's eastern border at Pelusium, to rescue Epiphanes. The Alexandrian mob took care of Agathocles and his sister by lynching them. When Epiphanes was twelve years old, it was decided that he should be crowned at Memphis, the ancient capital city of Egypt, rather than in Alexandria. In 196 BC, the good things that the king, it was claimed, had done for Egypt were recorded by the priests of Memphis and inscribed on a black basalt stone in the two languages spoken in the country, Greek and Egyptian, and in three scripts: Greek, demotic (the everyday script of the Egyptians) and hieroglyphic (used for important or religious records). The stone is known today as the Rosetta Stone, after the place in the western Nile Delta where it was discovered in AD 1799. It is now in the British Museum.

In 192 BC, Ptolemy V Epiphanes sealed the peace that had been made between Egypt and Syria by marrying Cleopatra I, daughter of Antiochus III. They had two sons, both, confusingly, named Ptolemy, and a daughter, Cleopatra, and when Epiphanes died in 180 BC, the elder boy succeeded him as Ptolemy VI Philometor ('Mother-loving', 180-145 BC). Like his father before him, he was a child at his accession, and so his mother acted as regent until her death five years later. Cleopatra I was a capable ruler who made a determined effort to erode the barriers between her Greek and Egyptian subjects by encouraging them to work together and to intermarry. Outside Alexandria, many Greeks took up an Egyptian way of life. Unfortunately, Cleopatra I's highly successful regency lasted for only five years before she died, leaving her son, and Egypt, in the hands of two ambitious officials, this time Lenaeus and Eulaeus, who appointed themselves guardians of the young king. In 170 BC, they demanded that Ptolemy's uncle, Antiochus IV of Syria, return Coele-Syria to Egyptian control, but Antiochus launched a preemptive strike against Egypt, conquering large parts of the country, though not Alexandria, and capturing Ptolemy VI Philometor. Antiochus allowed Ptolemy VI to continue ruling as a puppet king and withdrew back to Syria. Once Antiochus had departed, Alexandria chose a new king, Ptolemy's younger brother, who ruled as Ptolemy VIII Euergetes II (170-163 BC and 145-116). The two brothers chose not to fight a civil war but agreed to rule Egypt jointly instead. Rome decreed that the elder Ptolemy should rule in Memphis and the younger brother in Alexandria, alongside his sister, Cleopatra II. Ptolemy VI Philometor was killed in battle in 145 BC, leaving his young son, Ptolemy VII Neos ('New') Philopator, at the mercy of his uncle, Euergetes II. In an attempt to protect her son's interests, Cleopatra II agreed to marry her brother, Euergetes II: but as soon as she bore him a son of his own, Euergetes II had Neos Philopator put to death.

Euergetes II became besotted with his ambitious niece, Cleopatra, daughter of his sister-wife, Cleopatra II. She agreed to marry him on condition that she was given the same status as her mother, and so became Cleopatra III: a distinction was made between the two queens, one being characterised as 'Cleopatra the Sister' and the other as 'Cleopatra the Wife'. Although Euergetes II was a repulsive figure known to the Alexandrians as 'Physkon' ('Pot-belly'), the marriage was not one in name only: Cleopatra III was to bear him five children. Euergetes II rapidly became a highly unpopular ruler, so much so that in 163 BC he was forced to flee to Cyprus, taking with him Cleopatra III and their children, and Memphites (of Memphis), his son by Cleopatra II. When she claimed sole possession of the throne, Euergetes II had their son, Memphites, killed. The child's dismembered body was put into a chest and sent to his mother as a birthday present.

After some eighteen years in exile in Cyprus, Euergetes II had amassed an army strong enough for him to invade Egypt and reclaim the throne. For a time, Cleopatra II ruled jointly with her daughter and the man who had murdered her son; but it is unclear how long she survived and whether she died a natural death. When Euergetes II died in 116 BC, Cleopatra III inherited Egypt as stipulated in his will. Their eldest son, Ptolemy IX Soter II, known as 'Lathyros' or 'Chickpea', a man of about twenty-five years of age, was elected joint ruler with his mother. She, however, preferred his younger, more pliable brother, Alexander, and, after several failed attempts, managed to drive Soter II into exile, whereupon her favoured son became king as Ptolemy X Alexander I (110-101 and 107-88 BC). The reigns of both kings were bedevilled by the ambitions of their mother.

Ptolemy X Alexander I ruled jointly with Cleopatra III until her death at the age of sixty in 101 BC, a death that may have been engineered by her ungrateful son. Alexander was a repulsive figure: he was so obese that he was unable to walk unaided. Nevertheless, his niece, Cleopatra Berenice, the daughter of the exiled Soter II, was prepared to marry him. He was highly unpopular with the Egyptians, who forced him to flee Alexandria. When he died in a naval battle 88 BC, Soter II regained the throne and for the next seven years ruled jointly with Cleopatra Berenice. In 80 BC, Soter II was succeeded by his nephew, Ptolemy XI Alexander II, son of Alexander I. Alexander II had been a minor prince of the royal family, a protégé of the all-powerful Roman general, Sulla, who propelled him to the throne. On his death he left a will, in all probability forged, in which he bequeathed Egypt to Rome. Rome at first declined to intervene in Egyptian affairs, and it was not until 67 BC that it ordered Pompey (see page 40) to clear the Mediterranean of the pirates from Cilicia (modern Turkey) who were interfering with Alexandria's trade and seriously impeding Rome's food supply. His reign lasted for less than a year: having married and, nineteen days later, killed Cleopatra Berenice, he was murdered by an Alexandrian mob. He had no sons and the throne of Egypt passed to an illegitimate son of Soter II and an Alexandrian Greek woman whose name is unknown. He was proclaimed king as Ptolemy XII Neos Dionysos (80-58 and 55-51 BC) and married his sister, Cleopatra IV Tryphaena, a daughter of Soter II and a mistress.

The new king's second name - the new Dionysus - was appropriate: Dionysus was the Greek god of, amongst other things, wine and music, two things of which Neos Dionysus was inordinately fond. The Alexandrians immediately gave Neos Dionysos a nickname, 'Nothus' (Bastard), but when they discovered his fondness for flute-playing they renamed him 'Auletes' (Piper). Auletes, who needed the patronage of Rome in order to proceed with his coronation, sought to obtain it by means of bribery, confident that Egypt's resources were limitless. He was mistaken. Receipts from crown monopolies such as the gold mines of Nubia and the Eastern Desert, had dwindled; Cyprus, which was ruled by his younger brother, Ptolemy, was making little contribution to the exchequer; Cyrenaica no longer paid tribute; the linen industry was moribund; and farmers had become reluctant to send their produce to Alexandria for fear of not being paid. Fortunately for Auletes, Alexandria decided that the illegitimacy of an uncrowned king could not be countenanced and that the coronation of Auletes should proceed with or without the support of Rome.

During his reign, Auletes attempted to secure his hold on the Egyptian throne and to safeguard his children's inheritance by adopting a pro-Roman policy. In 63 BC, he tried to gain the support of Pompey, by then one of the most powerful men in Rome, by sending him gifts of money and valuables and extending an invitation to him to visit Alexandria. Pompey accepted the gifts but declined the invitation. A short time later, Auletes arrived in Rome seeking an official recognition of his kingship. After paying a bribe of six thousand talents to Julius Caesar and Pompey, a formal alliance was agreed and Auletes was recognised as a 'friend and ally' of the people of Rome. In 58 BC, Auletes failed to make any protest against the Roman conquest of Cyprus. This, and the resentment of the Egyptians who were burdened by the heavy taxes being levied to pay for the bribe, led to rioting and Auletes judged it prudent to seek sanctuary in Rome, taking his eleven-year-old daughter, Cleopatra, with him, and leaving his wife, Cleopatra VI Tryphania, to rule Egypt in his absence. Auletes had five children, three were daughters: Berenice, born in 76 BC, Cleopatra, born in about 69 BC and Arsinoe, born in about 63 BC. In 61 BC and 59 BC his sons were born, both named Ptolemy.

Tryphania chose her daughter Berenice to rule Egypt with her, which she did as Berenice IV (58-55 BC), but within two years Tryphania was ousted by Berenice's husband, Archelaus. Berenice attempted to reconcile the Egyptians with the Crown, and Archelaus made a start on reforming the army and refitting the navy, but their efforts were cut short in 55 BC when the proconsul of Syria, Aulus Gabinius, restored Auletes to the throne. Auletes imprisoned his daughter and her husband, and had them murdered. Four years later, he died. Before his death, Auletes elevated his daughter, Cleopatra, to share the throne with him and in his will he explicitly declared that she and her brother, the elder Ptolemy, should become husband and wife and rule Egypt together. To safeguard their interests, he requested the Roman Senate to deposit a copy of his will in the Republic's archives. Pompey, his chief ally, was named executor.

On the death of her father in 51 BC, the eighteen-year-old Cleopatra became queen-regnant of Egypt as Cleopatra VII Philopator ('Father-loving') and married her ten-year-old brother, the elder of the two named Ptolemy, who thus became Ptolemy XIII Theos Philopator ('Father-loving God') (51-47 BC). Cleopatra could look to her own female ancestors for inspiration. Her male ancestors have been described as 'virile if not especially virtuous rulers'[4] They had a propensity for murdering each other, an activity in which many of their queens, sisters, wives and daughters, all called Arsinoe, Berenice or Cleopatra, were prepared to match the men. They, like the men, were ruthlessly ambitious.

Arsinoe II, not only the wife but also the sister of Ptolemy II Philadelphus, set the bar fairly high when it came to the political power that could be enjoyed by a Ptolemaic queen. Presumably due to the high opinion of her held by her husband, she was represented on monuments almost as though she were a king. For about seven years of Ptolemy II's reign, she exerted great influence. As though she were a king, a royal titulary (see page 276) was established for her, one which set the pattern for subsequent queens. She was 'Sovereign of the Two Lands (Egypt), She Who Brings the King Delight, She Whom the Gods Love, Daughter of Amun, Lady of the Diadems, Arsinoe, Who Loves Her Brother, Who Pleases Maat (the goddess of Truth and Justice)'. Both before and after her death, Arsinoe II was identified with Isis, the sister-wife of Osiris, ruler of the Afterlife; and when she died, her brother-husband dedicated temples to her.

Arsinoe II had raised in her own household her husband's children by his first wife, Arsinoe, daughter of the powerful King of Thrace, Lysimachus. The elder son of this marriage, who became king as Ptolemy III Euergetes, married Berenice, the daughter of King Magus of Cyrenaica and the third queen to bear the name Berenice. She became the beneficiary of a further transformation in the role of queen, as illustrated in temple reliefs in which she was depicted standing behind the king as he performed the ritual. Since the king alone was permitted to carry out these sacred acts (at least, in theory, in practice, the king could not be everywhere at once, so could be represented by the high priest of the temple) this was unheard of, except in the most iconoclastic period of Egyptian history, the reign of Akhenaten (1350-1334 BC), the so-called heretic pharaoh who permitted his wife, Nefertiti, to be depicted in temple reliefs standing alongside him while he performed the ritual. Berenice III took the title 'female Horus' and in some documents she was even called per-aat or 'female pharaoh'.[5]

It would seem that many queens of the Ptolemaic dynasty were ready to 'lie back and think of England (or rather, Egypt)'[6] when it came to advantageous marriages. They were prepared to marry kings regardless of consanguinity and no matter how repugnant a king might be in appearance and actions: Cleopatra II could even bring herself to rule alongside the man who had murdered her son. Cleopatra VII, however, had long known that she was to be queen regnant: her father had trained her for the position. True, he had insisted on recognising his son by stipulating that he should rule alongside his sister; but Cleopatra was in no doubt that she was the senior partner, not only literally but in practice. Unlike the previous queens of the dynasty, she did not sit on the throne of Egypt by virtue of the fact that she had married a male relative, but was confident of the fact that she was entitled in her own right to be there.

On his return from Rome, Auletes had placed his elder son under the care of a Greek eunuch named Pothinus, who, like many eunuchs before and after him, dabbled in palace intrigue. Supported by his chief allies at court, the royal tutor, Theodotus, a Greek rhetorician, and the commander of the palace troops, an unscrupulous Egyptian soldier named Achillas, Pothinus saw his chance to rule Egypt in the name of the king. Cleopatra, however, was of the opinion that she should rule alone until her young brother came of age on his fifteenth birthday. Pothinus insisted that a woman could not rule without male support, ignoring the fact that several had done so, and suggested that he should rule in the name of Ptolemy with Cleopatra in a subordinate role. Once again, the Alexandrians stepped in and insisted that the two sides should learn to work together or hand over to others who would. Cleopatra and Pothinus agreed to divide authority: she would handle foreign relations, he would take care of domestic affairs. She probably realised that the actions of her father had rendered Egypt into a client state of Rome, and that the fate of client states was liable to be absorption into the ever-expanding Roman Empire. Cleopatra was to spend the whole of her reign endeavouring to prevent this happening.

It did not take long for Pothinus and his allies to realise that Cleopatra was, although a mere woman, never going to be amenable to their plans: she had a mind of her own and, above all, had been trained by her father to be a queen. Waiting in the wings was a replacement - her younger sister, Arsinoe - if they could just eliminate Cleopatra. Realising what was afoot, Cleopatra fled Alexandria and in 48 BC sought refuge in Syria - a not very auspicious beginning to the reign of a woman who was to become the greatest ruler of the Ptolemaic Dynasty and one of the greatest rulers in Egyptian history.

CHAPTER THREE

CLEOPATRA AND CAESAR

Once in Syria, a determined and resourceful Cleopatra began to rally support and to raise an army with which she could invade Egypt. Meanwhile, in Rome, the final decades of the Roman Republic, which for years had been ruled by a coalition of three men, Pompey, Crassus and Julius Caesar, were coming to an end.

Gnaeus Pompeius Magnus (106-48 BC), better known as Pompey, was one of the most successful generals of his age. In the late seventies BC he was commanded by the Roman Senate to bring Hispania (Spain) back under their control, and having accomplished this, he returned to Italy, where, in 71 BC, he was instrumental in quashing the slave revolt led by Spartacus. When the Senate ordered him to make an end to the menace of the Cilician pirates (Cicilia on the south coast of Asia Minor enjoyed easily defensible natural harbours), he was given a command that was meant to last for a period of three years. It took only three months for Pompey to deal with the pirates, and he decided to go on to pacify the eastern

Mediterranean. In 64 BC, he took control of Syria in the name of the Roman Republic and captured Jerusalem. When he returned to Rome in 61 BC, he was awarded a triumph. Two years later, he cemented an alliance with Julius Caesar by agreeing to take Caesar's daughter, Julia, as his wife. He was thirty years older than his seventeen-year-old bride, and the marriage, his fourth, was undertaken for political reasons, but it was to prove a happy union, with both parties being devoted to each other until the death, four years later, of Julia in childbirth at the age of only twenty-two.

Marcus Licinius Crassus (*c.* 115-53 BC) was a Roman general and politician who became the political and financial patron of Julius Caesar. He began his career as a military commander under Lucius Cornelius Sulla (138-79 BC), a politician and general who was victorious in the first full-scale civil war in Roman history (88–82 BC), after which he became dictator (82–79 BC), setting a precedent for Julius Caesar to follow. Under Sulla's dictatorship, Crassus amassed a huge fortune, largely due to property speculation: after Caesar Augustus, he is thought to have been the richest man in Roman history. He claimed that it was he, not Pompey, who defeated Spartacus. Crassus' deficiencies as a military commander were to be exposed during his campaign against the Parthian Empire, Rome's long-time enemy in the east, in what is now Iran, which was a disastrous failure, resulting in his defeat and death at the Battle of Carrhae.

Gaius Julius Caesar (100-44 BC) was not only a politician and one of the greatest military commanders in history, he was also a notable author of Latin prose. Although he was a patrician, a member of the ancient aristocracy of Rome, he allied himself with the Popular Party (Populares, that is, 'favouring the people'), a group which represented the plebeians (commoners), especially the urban poor, rather than with the Optimates ('Best Ones'), the group which promoted the interests of patricians and supported the Senate, Rome's chief governing and advisory body which was comprised chiefly of members from a small, hereditary, aristocracy. In 60 BC, Caesar, Crassus and Pompey formed the unofficial political alliance known as the First Triumvirate that was to dominate the Roman political system for several years. Their attempts to amass power as Populares were opposed by the Optimates in the Senate, among them Cato the Younger, who tried to preserve the Roman Republic against power seekers such as Julius Caesar; and Cicero, the great orator, writer and statesman. The alliance between the three men was not destined to last long: their egos and ambitions inevitably led to jealous rivalry. Caesar and Crassus were long-standing allies, but Crassus and Pompey disliked each other: the former resented the fact that the latter had taken credit for putting down the Spartacus rebellion. Caesar, however, persuaded Crassus that the alliance with Pompey was necessary in the furtherance of their political ambitions.

Shortly after the formation of the First Triumvirate, Caesar embarked upon the conquest of Gaul, which he completed in 51 BC. His commentaries on the campaign, and on the later civil war, are acknowledged to be masterpieces: he was a good historian despite that fact that his accounts showed him in the most favourable light. His military achievements were such that they gained him unprecedented military power and led to Pompey becoming increasingly envious of his success.

On the death of Crassus in 53 BC, the First Triumvirate had been broken, and Pompey supported the Senate when it ordered Caesar to step down from his military command and return to Rome. Caesar refused the order, and in 49 BC, without the permission of the Senate, led the 13th Legion across the Rubicon, the small river separating Gaul from Italy, illegally bringing an army into Italy with the words 'the die is cast'. In the civil war that ensued, Caesar and Pompey faced each other at the head of their respective armies. Caesar pursued his rival general to northern Greece and, on 9 August, 48 BC, defeated him at the Battle of Pharsalus. Pompey was forced to seek refuge in Egypt, leaving his conqueror in an unrivalled position of power.

In Egypt, the young king Ptolemy, with his advisors and his army, was stationed in the fortress at Pelusium on the eastern extreme of the Nile Delta, some 30 km (18 miles) south east of the modern Port Said. They were ready to oppose Cleopatra who was approaching Pelusium with the army of mercenaries that she had raised in a very short time in Syria. Pompey arrived at Alexandria expecting that the children of Auletes would offer him the same hospitality as he had once shown their father. On being told that Ptolemy and Cleopatra were making ready for battle, he sailed round to Pelusium. Pompey's arrival in Egypt, on 28 September, brought the first confirmation of his defeat at Pharsalus. The Alexandrians sided with him as he had, after all, always represented their interests in Rome; and Pompey might have hoped that with the support of an army raised in Egypt he could take back power from Caesar. However, some of Ptolemy's councillors had decided that Caesar was in the ascendant and that if the

Egyptians offered Pompey support they would be backing the wrong horse. Pompey was a loser and anyone with any sense did not back a loser. They advised the king not to offer sanctuary to Pompey but to request him politely to seek it elsewhere.

Theodotus went further. In a well reasoned speech - he was, after all, a professional rhetorician - he suggested that Ptolemy should curry favour with Caesar by having Pompey killed. The king readily agreed and Achillas was given the task of carrying out the murder. Septimius, a Roman officer who had once held command under Pompey, volunteered to help him and the two men were rowed out in a small boat to Pompey's galley, which was lying a short distance off shore. Once there, they invited Pompey aboard their boat, assuring him that it was the only way to come ashore due to the shallowness of the water. Although Pompey was suspicious, he had no choice but to agree; he could not even sail away for he could see that ships of the Egyptian navy were cruising in the vicinity. As he boarded Achillas' boat, Cornelia, his fifth wife, whom he had married four years earlier, made to accompany him, but he told her to wait on board the galley until she saw what happened to him on shore.

Pompey did not reach the shore alive. Before the boat was beached, Achillas and Septimius had stabbed him to death and cut off his head. Cornelia witnessed the murder and ordered the captain of the galley to weigh anchor and sail away. Pompey's body was bundled into the sea and his murderers carried his head to Ptolemy. A freedman named Philip, who had accompanied Pompey ashore, managed to retrieve his body. He gathered driftwood from the shore and, aided by Cordus, an old Roman soldier who had once served under Pompey, built a funerary pyre for Pompey the Great, the man whom 'Fortune had held in her arms so long and then destroyed with a single blow.'[1]

A few days later, Julius Caesar arrived at Alexandria. Theodotus, confident of Caesar's gratitude for the dispatch of his enemy, came on board his ship, carrying with him Pompey's head and signet ring. He was sorely mistaken: Caesar turned away in disgust at the sight of the head and, taking the ring in his hand, shed tears for the death of a great Roman, his erstwhile son-in-law, at the hands of villainous men on the make. He curtly dismissed Theodotus from his presence; and it was not long before the scheming royal tutor had fled Egypt. Some years later, he was captured by Marcus Brutus, who deplored his murder of a man seeking sanctuary and had Theodotus crucified. It is very likely that Caesar would not have had Pompey executed but sent into exile. Out of respect for his great rival, he had his ashes conveyed to Cornelia, who had them interred at Pompey's country estate near Alba; and gave orders that his head be buried in a grove just beyond Alexandria's eastern wall in a shrine dedicated to Nemesis, the Greek goddess of retribution. Caesar did not seek retribution from Pompey's followers but pardoned them: he was always magnanimous in victory, at least towards lesser men - their leaders were a different matter.

Caesar's presence was needed in Rome, to settle things down after the turmoil of his struggle against Pompey. Instead, he elected to stay in Egypt. It was only after his arrival in the country that he was fully informed of the parlous state of affairs between the two sibling rulers, and that Cleopatra was at the head of an army outside Pelusium. He decided that it was his duty to reconcile them before he left Egypt; and besides, he had given Auletes his support in return for a bribe which, as was usual with Auletes, had never been paid. Since his children were held responsible for their father's debts, there was a good chance of Caesar being able to collect on the debt, an attractive proposition since he was a spendthrift who was always short of money. At this time, Caesar was a man in his early fifties who had spent decades fighting in foreign countries: a period of rest and recuperation in a beautiful palace overlooking that Mediterranean must have had a certain appeal. He decided to take up residence in the Royal Palace on the Lochias Promontory in Alexandria, which was unoccupied save for the younger Ptolemy and his sister, Arsinoe, and a few servants.

In September 48 BC, Caesar made a state entry into Alexandria accompanied by four thousand troops, with the *fasces*, the bundle of rods enclosing an axe that symbolised Roman authority, carried before them. It must have seemed to the Alexandrians that here at last Rome had accomplished what she had for so long threatened, the conquest of Egypt. The city was in a ferment at this insult to the royal family and in the rioting that ensued several of Caesar's soldiers were killed. Caesar was fairly sure that the Alexandrians would not go to war with him, but he took no chances and sent to Asia Minor for reinforcements, a wise precaution since the citizens of Alexandria were becoming ever more resentful at the cost of feeding and paying for their uninvited guests.

Ptolemy and Cleopatra were summoned to leave Pelusium and travel home to Alexandria to present their cases to Caesar.

Ptolemy arrived at the Palace accompanied by Pothinus, and was courteously received by Caesar. He lectured the boy on the benefits of family unity, explained to him that he was intending to arbitrate between him and his sister, and asked the young king where that sister was. He then turned to Pothinus to complain about the weevil-infested wheat and rancid oil that was being given to his soldiers, and demanded to know the reason for the non-payment of Auletes' debts. Pothinus retorted that he had better things to think about than army rations; and that he would have to scrutinise the details of Auletes' debt before it could be paid. He added that he did not control Cleopatra's movements. Caesar realised that the queen would not be given safe passage if Pothinus had anything to do with it, and ordered him not to leave the city.

Meanwhile, Cleopatra was making her way back to Alexandria. She took ship from Pelusium and twenty-four hours later, aboard a small boat, was rowed by her servant, a Sicilian named Apollodorus, into the Great Port. There they waited until darkness fell. Cleopatra knew that she could not enter the Palace openly for fear that her brother and his backers would arrange for her to have a fatal accident. She must have known the Palace like the back of her hand and been familiar with its secret passages, so it was relatively easy for her to make her way through the building unseen. She may even have visited her own rooms to tidy herself up after the sea journey, and to change out of her dishevelled clothes into a clean dress before making her way to the section of the Palace that Caesar had chosen as his quarters. It is thought today that is it extremely unlikely that she was smuggled into

Caesar's presence wrapped in a carpet (see page 138) but her first meeting with the man who was to become her lover was in private.

Julius Caesar was known to be a womaniser: the list of his mistresses is a long one, and included queens other than Cleopatra and the wives of many of his fellow officers and friends. This incorrigible rake even seduced the wives of Crassus and Pompey at a time when he needed the support of their husbands. He had three wives: the first was Cornelia, the sister of Lucius Cornelius Cinna, a leader of the Populares Party, whom he married in 84 BC. She bore him his only legitimate child, a daughter, Julia (who was to marry Pompey) and died giving birth to a stillborn son in 69 BC. Two years later, Caesar married Pompeia, whose mother was the daughter of Sulla. Caesar was elected Pontifex Maximus, or high priest of the state religion, in 63 BC, and a year later Pompeia acted as hostess during the festival of the Bona Dea (good goddess) which was held in the official residence on the Via Sacra in Rome. No men were permitted to attend this festival, but a young patrician named Publius Clodius Pulcher disguised himself as a woman and gained entry to the house, allegedly in order to seduce Pompeia. He was caught and prosecuted for sacrilege. Caesar declined to give evidence at the trial, and Clodius was acquitted. Nevertheless, Caesar divorced Pompeia on the grounds that a wife of his should never be under suspicion, giving rise to the saying, 'Caesar's wife must be above suspicion,' with the more general meaning that if one is involved with a famous or prominent figure, one must avoid attracting negative attention. Caesar then married Calpurnia, the daughter of Lucius Calpurnius

Piso Caesoninus, consul in 58 BC. They stayed married until Caesar's death, after which Calpurnia remained a widow for the rest of her life. Caesar's marriages were undertaken to cement alliances or gain valuable dowries. The woman who was closest to him was Servilia, a patrician who was married to a complaisant husband. She was more or less the same age as Caesar and was a woman of the world with many useful political contacts. Caesar trusted her judgement. He lavished presents upon her, including pearls of immense value; it was even rumoured that he undertook his expedition to Britain in 55 BC not as a reconnaissance prior to mounting an invasion of the island but because he had heard that pearls of very good quality could be obtained there. Servilia was the mother of Marcus Junius Brutus, who may or may not have been Caesar's son, but was certainly to become one of Caesar's assassins.

According to the Roman historian, Dion Cassius, Caesar was spellbound the moment he set eyes on Cleopatra and she opened her mouth to speak. Nobody can know the truth of this, of course - the meeting was, after all, in private. But it is not hard to imagine that Caesar was impressed by the courage and determination it would have taken for the young queen to have made her way alone into his presence. He had known many women, but none of them had been queen regnant of a country, even if Cleopatra was yet to cement her authority. Addressing him in Latin in her beautiful, seductive voice, she probably set about convincing him of the righteousness of her cause; and perhaps it did not take long for Caesar to recognise that here was a woman after his own heart. His wives were dutiful Roman matrons, his mistresses had provided sexual gratification, but Cleopatra was his intellectual equal. Given Caesar's reputation with women, it is more than probable that he seduced the queen, who was almost young enough to be his granddaughter, that night; and that she was more than willing to be seduced. The wellspring for part of this love story is of course simply described: she was attracted to Caesar because he was the most powerful man in the world; he was attracted to her because she was the richest woman.

When the young king Ptolemy was summoned into Caesar's presence, he found his sister comfortably ensconced. Jumping to the conclusion that he was the loser in his struggle against Cleopatra, Ptolemy rushed from the room in tears. Pothinus began stirring up the Alexandrian mob, but Caesar confronted them outside the palace, carrying the copy of Auletes' will that had been retained in Alexandria. He read the document to them, paragraph by paragraph, and announced that it was his decision, as Consul of Egypt, that the terms of the will should be observed and that the elder Ptolemy and Cleopatra should marry and share joint rulership of Egypt, as their father had intended. As a gesture of goodwill, he decreed that Cyprus should be restored to Egypt and that the younger Ptolemy and his sister, Arsinoe, should govern it together.

Caesar's proposal was to no avail. Pothinus had still not given up hope that Ptolemy XIII could somehow manage to oust Cleopatra, and was again stirring up the Alexandrian mob. He was arrested and put into prison where, on Cleopatra's orders, he was strangled. Meanwhile, Achillas and an army of 20,000 men were laying siege to the palace. Caesar managed to defend his stronghold and gave orders for the Egyptian fleet to be burnt. In the ensuing conflagration, the Great Library caught fire and was badly damaged. After some months under siege, Caesar led an attempt to capture the Pharos. He was unsuccessful and at one point had to jump into the water and swim to safety. Plutarch says that he swam with one hand, using the other to hold some important despatches above his head to keep them dry. Suetonius adds that he towed his general's purple cloak, holding it in his teeth, so that it would not fall into the hands of the Egyptians.

During Achillas' siege of Alexandria, the sixteen-year-old Arsinoe escaped and joined him. At first, she was welcome: but she soon began to behave with typical Ptolemaic arrogance, demanding to be treated as a queen - which she was, though only of Cyprus - and countermanding his orders. She had him killed and replaced him at the head of the Egyptian army with Ganymedes, her chamberlain. Ganymedes enjoyed some success in fighting Caesar's troops, but eventually Caesar negotiated an end to the fighting by exchanging Ptolemy for Arsinoe. The king immediately took command of the Egyptians; but Caesar, reinforced by two Roman legions and the army of his ally, King Mithridates of Pergamum, outmanoeuvred the Ptolemaic forces, and on 26 March (13 January in the modern calendar) 47 BC, the king was killed, probably by drowning in the Nile as he attempted to flee across the river in an overladen boat. Arsinoe was sent to Rome, where, in 46 BC, she suffered the humiliation of being led in Caesar's Triumph (see page 62). Although it was the custom to execute prominent personages after a Triumph was over, Caesar spared Arsinoe and had her conveyed to Ephesus. She found sanctuary in the Temple of Diana, where she lived an uneasy life never knowing when her sister would send assassins to kill her.

Caesar had now spent six months in Egypt. Matters were not going well in Rome and needed his attention. Nevertheless, he elected to stay in Egypt and with Cleopatra set off on a Nile cruise. This was part pleasure and part propaganda, with a dash of business interests. The story had been circulated that Caesar was the incarnation of the state god of Egypt, Amun. In this, he went one better than Alexander, who had only claimed to be the son of Amun. Cleopatra had long been identified with the goddess Isis. According to Egyptian mythology, Isis was the wife of Osiris, the divine king of Egypt who was killed and dismembered by his brother, Seth. Isis collected the pieces of his body and reassembled it, enabling Osiris to become ruler of the Afterlife. She bore him a son, Horus, whom she protected until he was old enough to claim his rightful place upon the throne of Egypt. Isis was revered as a wife and mother; and it was said that the tears she shed over the murdered Osiris' body formed the river Nile. The cruise was an opportunity to display the two living deities to the Egyptian people.

The royal barge that conveyed Caesar and Cleopatra up the Nile was a splendid vessel. Athenaeus, the Greek writer who was born in Naucratis, in the western Delta, described it as being over 90 metres (300 feet) long and some 14 metres (45 feet) in the beam. It rose nearly 90 metres (60 feet) above the water, and was propelled by several banks of oars. The royal barge was not so much a ship as a palace, for, like a palace, it contained banqueting rooms and courtyards, as well as bedrooms; it even had gardens and shrines. Although

Athenaeus was writing over two centuries later, he based his description on the work of earlier historians, and his is probably an accurate account of a Ptolemaic state barge. A large fleet of vessels - the historian Appian claimed that there were four hundred of them - followed behind, bringing supplies and conveying hundreds of troops to ensure that the cruise went smoothly. Appian recorded that Caesar explored the country in the company of Cleopatra, 'generally enjoying himself with her'. The fleet halted its progress at Denderah, so that the queen could make offerings to the goddess, Hathor; and went on to Thebes (modern Luxor) where she had the vessel moored on the western bank at Hermonthis (modern Armant), so that she could preside over the installation of the new Bukhis Bull, the living bull that was housed in a shrine and thought to be the incarnation of the war god, Montu. All this time, Caesar, a man of insatiable curiosity, was enjoying the scenery and the splendours of ancient temples; but he was also weighing up the richness of the land, its extreme fertility and the ability of the population of Upper (southern) Egypt to pay the taxation that was necessary for the public buildings that he could see on the banks of the Nile. It could even be that he was told of Ethiopia, the land of gold and ivory and exotic animals; and maybe he dreamed of one day emulating Alexander and reaching India, not by travelling overland as Alexander had done but by sailing down the Red Sea from an Ethiopian port.

Perhaps the most important aim of the journey up the Nile was to display Caesar and Cleopatra as divine consorts, for Cleopatra was now pregnant. Caesar's wife, Calpurnia, awaited him in Rome, and at this point he seemingly saw no advantage in divorcing her in order to marry the Egyptian queen. In the eyes of the Egyptians, however, he was already married to Cleopatra. According to Egyptian custom, there was no ceremony of marriage: a woman merely moved into the house of her prospective husband and by doing so was recognised as his wife. Technically, it was Caesar who had moved into the house of Cleopatra, but the effect was the same. The Egyptians had no problems with him being married to Calpurnia: in Egyptian law a man was allowed take more then one wife at a time, especially if his existing wife, like Calpurnia, had borne him no children. In effect, Caesar was King of Egypt - uncrowned, presumably by his own choice. Since the overthrow of the tyrannical king, Tarquinius Superbus, in the late sixth century BC, Romans had had an antipathy towards monarchy. Caesar, however, had begun to display monarchical tendencies, and it is not hard to imagine that Cleopatra envisioned the day when he would make himself King of Rome. Together, they would rule the Roman Empire and Egypt, and the Roman Empire and Egypt would rule the world.

On his return to Alexandria, Caesar received news that Pharnaces, the King of Pontus, a region on the southern Black Sea coast of modern Turkey, had taken advantage of the Civil War in Rome and was extending his dominions. The news precipitated Caesar's departure from Egypt. Before he left, he took steps to consolidate Cleopatra's position. He bound her brother, the younger Ptolemy, to her by making him her co-ruler as Ptolemy XIV, considering that the boy, who was only about twelve years old, would prove no threat to his older, stronger sister, who would be able to prevent him falling under the influence of her enemies. He left behind three legions under the command of his trusted legate, Rufinus. In June 47 BC, Caesar left Alexandria and marched towards Pontus. Two months later, he routed Pharnaces and wrote to his friend, Amantius, declaring 'veni, vidi, vici' - 'I came, I saw, I conquered.' Two months after that, in October, 47 BC, Caesar arrived back in Rome, only to leave again within weeks, forced to sail for North Africa to deal with an Optimates army, led by Cato, who had made an alliance with King Juba I of Numidia. The Optimates were decisively defeated at Thapsus, after which Cato committed suicide rather than submit to being pardoned by Caesar. When the victorious and now unchallenged Caesar arrived back in Rome, he was named Dictator for ten years and awarded his third consulship.

Either immediately before or soon after Caesar left Egypt, Cleopatra bore a son, whom she named Ptolemy Caesar claiming that he was the son of Caesar. The Alexandrians nicknamed the child Caesarion or 'Little Caesar' and that became the name by which he was known. In July, 46 BC, Caesar sent for Cleopatra and the year-old Caesarion. Aware of the Ptolemaic family tradition, he also summoned the young King Ptolemy XIV, just in case he and his supporters took advantage of Cleopatra's absence to oust her from the throne. Cleopatra arrived in Rome with an impressively large retinue and was established in a luxurious villa surrounded by beautiful gardens on the right bank of the Tiber, near the modern Villa Doria Pamphili.

One of the purposes of Cleopatra's visit to Rome was to witness the celebration of Caesar's Triumph, which lasted for four days, the longest and most splendid that Rome had ever seen. On the first day, Caesar processed through the city, acknowledging the plaudits of the crowd. At the end of the parade, his victory over Gaul was marked by the execution of Vercingetorix, the Gaulish chieftain who had resisted him valiantly but had in the end surrendered to save his fellow Gauls from further punishment. Such executions were customary at the end of a Triumph, but it was mean-spirited of Caesar that he did not spare such an honourable enemy. On the second day, his victory in Egypt was celebrated. Princess Arsinoe was led through the streets in chains, no doubt to the delight of her sister, Cleopatra. It would not have been good policy to have executed the sister of the Egyptian queen, so, presumably to the chagrin of that queen, Arsinoe was spared. On the third day, the conquest of Pontus was celebrated; and on the fourth, the victories in North Africa. The fact that the Queen of Egypt was an honoured guest at the Triumph was meant to be seen as an acknowledgment that Caesar had not conquered Egypt but only those who had rebelled against him and the queen.

Caesar was to celebrate one more Triumph. In April, 45 BC, the two sons of Pompey the Great, Gnaeus and Sextus, led a revolt in Spain. Caesar defeated them at Munda. Gnaeus Pompey was killed in battle but his brother escaped and eventually set up a base in Sicily. In October that year, Caesar celebrated a Triumph to mark his victory over Gnaeus Pompey. Many Romans considered this a Triumph too far, since such events were meant to celebrate victories over foreign enemies, not citizens of Rome. Caesar courted further unpopularity by ordering that a statue of Cleopatra be placed in the temple of Venus Genetrix, the goddess whom he claimed as his divine ancestress. Because of this claimed divine ancestry, he allowed his statues, especially those in the provinces, to be adorned as though they were statues of gods.

Caesar now reigned supreme in Rome. He ruled autocratically, often simply announcing his decisions to the Senate, rather in the manner of the executive orders that American presidents sometimes employ, and having them recorded as senatorial decrees with no debate or vote. His behaviour was eccentric. Doubtless encouraged by Cleopatra, he increasingly began to think of himself as not only a king but a god. His reach extended to the passage of time: possibly encouraged by Cleopatra, he decided to switch the Roman calendar from one calculated on the cycles of the moon to one based on the Egyptian, solar, model. The fifth month of the Roman year was renamed July in his honour. A further honour was bestowed upon him by the Lupercii, the order of priests responsible for conducting the Lupercalia, the ancient Roman fertility festival that was conducted annually on 15 February: they established a new college named the Lupercii Julii. He had been made Imperator, or commander-in-chief, an honour usually awarded to successful generals in the field of battle, which he undoubtedly richly deserved; but in Caesar's case the title came to mean Emperor or Monarch of an Empire. Caesar adopted it as a prefix to his name; and arranged that it should be handed on to his children and his children's children. As yet, he had no children who were legitimate in Roman eyes; but he had only to divorce Calpurnia, marry Cleopatra, and legitimise Caesarion, who was possibly the first of many children Cleopatra may bear him. It seems clear that he intended to establish a Julio-Ptolemaic dynasty, possibly with two capital cities, one, the fairly provincial Rome, the other the far more prosperous and splendid Alexandria. Caesar was now consumed with hubris: it could not be long before he was overtaken by nemesis.

Caesar was nearly fifty-six years old. He had led a hard, military life, dogged by sporadic episodes of 'the falling sickness', which was caused either by epilepsy or by mini strokes. He was prematurely aged: on a coin struck at this time, he is shown as a balding man with hollow cheeks and a wrinkled forehead; his neck is scrawny and he has a sagging dewlap. His behaviour was more that of a man in the grip of a mid-life crisis: he was prone to bouts of melancholy and preferred to listen to the words of flatterers. This did not stop the Senate constantly awarding him new honours such as the right to wear the laurel wreath and a purple and gold toga and to sit in a gilded chair at all public functions. In February, 44 BC, Caesar was named Dictator Perpetuus or Dictator for Life, the first in Roman history. On 15 February that year, Caesar presided over the feast of Lupercalia, seated in the Forum on a golden throne and wearing his purple and gold toga for the first time in public. Lupercus, after whom the feast was named, was identified with the nature god, Faunus or Pan, and represented the return of spring, the time of burgeoning plants and fecundity in women. During the festival, two young men belonging to the Order of Lupercus, cut the skins of sacrificial animals into strips, called *februa*, after which the month of February is named, and ran through the streets striking women with these *februa*. It was believed that any woman so struck would become pregnant during the following year.

At the Lupercalia of 44 BC, Mark Antony happened to be one of the Luperci. He bounded into the Forum followed by a large, enthusiastic crowd, and hailed Caesar as Lupercus himself. He then attempted to place a diadem, the symbol of Hellenistic monarchs, upon Caesar's head, to shouts of approval from various strategically placed supporters. The crowd, however, either stayed silent or voiced disapproval, and Caesar handed the diadem back to Antony. The diadem was offered again, and again Caesar, sensing the crowd's disapproval, refused it. The tumultuous applause that this elicited from the crowd resulted in Caesar ordering that the diadem be taken to the great Temple of Jupiter that stood on the Capitoline Hill overlooking the Forum and placed upon the head of the god's statue that stood within it; and that the incident be recorded in the public records as follows: 'On this day, acting on the wishes of the people, Mark Antony offered Caesar the royal crown but the Dictator refused to accept it.' Caesar, not to mention Cleopatra, must have been disappointed at this outcome, but both would have hoped that in time the Romans would accept him as king.

Even before the Lupercalia, a group of conspirators had begun to discuss the ways and means of ridding Rome of this Dictator who did 'bestride the narrow world like a Colossus'.[2] One of the leaders of the conspiracy was Gaius Cassius, an able general who had been one of Pompey's admirals. He was an ardent Republican who could not forgive Caesar for having pardoned him after Pompey's defeat: in his turn, Caesar did not trust Cassius who, he considered, in the words of Shakespeare, had 'a lean and hungry look' and thought too much: 'such men are dangerous'.[3] Cassius persuaded Marcus Junius Brutus to join him in the conspiracy, the same Brutus whom Caesar had always treated like a son, even giving orders that he not be harmed during the Battle of Pharsalus. Other conspirators included Gaius Trebonius, whom Caesar had just appointed Proconsul of Asia; Gaius Cassius Longinus, Brutus' brother-in-law; the two Casca brothers, Gaius Servilius, who was a close friend of Caesar, and Publius Servilius, whom Mark Antony characterised as 'envious'; and two men who had been confidants of Caesar, Tillius Cimber and Servus Galba. They justified their plot against Caesar by claiming that it was an idealistic attempt to return Rome to the days of the Republic; but several of them were self-seeking and had a personal hatred of the Dictator. They had pretended to share Caesar's plans, they had feigned friendship and saw him nearly every day, but still they plotted not just to overthrow him but to assassinate him.

On 15 March, 44 BC, the infamous Ides of March against which Caesar had been warned, he attended a meeting of the Senate, held not at the normal meeting house, which had been badly burned and was being rebuilt, but at its temporary quarters in the portico of the Curia, the theatre built by Pompey the Great in the Forum. Sixty conspirators, led by Marcus Junius Brutus and Gaius Cassius Longinus, came to the meeting with daggers concealed in their togas and struck Caesar at least twenty-three times as he stood at the base of Pompey's statue. Legend has it that the dying Caesar said to Brutus, 'Et tu, Brute!' ('Even you, Brutus!'), before covering his face with a fold of his toga, just as Pompey had done four years previously, and dying. After his death, all the senators fled, and several hours later, a group of slaves carried Caesar's body home to Calpurnia. For several days there was a political vacuum, for the conspirators apparently had not thought about what to do next and, in a major blunder, did not immediately seek out Mark Antony and try to kill him.

Mark Antony was now the most powerful man in Rome. He, with the support of his ally, Marcus Aemilius Lepidus (see page 69), had command of the legion that was quartered just outside the city: the conspirators had only a band of gladiators. Antony's position was further reinforced when Calpurnia entrusted him with her dead husband's will and personal documents, and, perhaps even more important, his private fortune and access to the state treasury. Antony was quick to publish the will: in it, every man in Rome was given three hundred sesterces; and Caesar's gardens beyond the Tiber were handed over to the city. Five days after his assassination, Caesar's body was carried to the Campus Martius, the Field of Mars, a publicly-owned stretch of land that lay between the city and the Tiber, where a great funerary pyre had been erected. The funeral cortege passed through the Forum and was placed at the foot of the Rostra, the platform from which speakers could address the Senate. Antony seized his moment when he was allowed to deliver the funerary eulogy, given wonderful expression by Shakespeare in *Julius Caesar*:

> Friends, Romans, countrymen, lend me your ears:
> I come to bury Caesar, not to praise him.
> The evil that men do lives after them:

The good is oft interr'd with their bones
So let it be with Caesar. The noble Brutus
Hath told you Caesar was ambitious:
If it were so, it was a grievous fault,
And grievously hath Caesar answered it.
Here, under leave of Brutus and the rest -
For Brutus is an honourable man:
So are they all, all honourable men -
Come I to speak in Caesar's funeral.
He was my friend, faithful and just to me;
But Brutus says he was ambitious,
And Brutus is an honourable man.[4]

Antony goes on to list the ways in which Caesar filled the coffers in Rome, wept when the poor cried, refused the crown that Antony offered him at the Lupercalia, telling the crowd that they all loved Caesar once and not without cause. Throughout the oration, he repeats the phrase 'Yet Brutus says he was ambitious', until finally he asks the crowd to bear with him for 'My heart is in the coffin there with Caesar, And I must pause till it come back to me.'

The powerful eulogy fanned the flames of popular feeling against the conspirators, and Brutus and Cassius were persuaded that their safest policy was to leave Rome. Antony then began to take steps to consolidate his position. Marcus Aemilius Lepidus (*c.*89-13 BC), a military commander and close ally of Caesar's, took his place as Pontifex Maximus, two of the conspirators were allowed to leave Rome and take up the positions in the provinces to which Caesar had appointed them - Trebonius in Asia and Decimus Brutus in Gaul. Antony introduced an agrarian bill that secured land for Caesar's army veterans; and appeased the Senate by suggesting that the dictatorship should be permanently abolished. He bided his time but he knew that one day he would have to deal with Brutus and Cassius.

Cleopatra must have heard of Caesar's murder soon after it had happened. Doubtless she grieved for her lover, for the end of their ambitions to found a Julio-Ptolemaic dynasty, for the realisation that they would never sit side by side on golden thrones. The position of their son, Caesarion, would not be regularised, he would not be recognised as Caesar's heir. All she could do was hope that Caesar's murderers would not come for her. It seems likely that she consulted Antony, Caesar's trusted lieutenant, who may have advised her to wait in Rome to see how things developed. It was not long, however, before she departed for Egypt, taking her son with her. It may have been at this juncture that Cleopatra saw that Antony was potentially Caesar's successor as leader of the Roman world, and started to make plans for him to take Caesar's place in her life. On her return to Egypt, she disposed of her young co-ruler, Ptolemy XIV, possibly by poisoning him with aconite, and in 43 BC, replaced him with the four-year-old Caesarion, who became joint ruler with her as Ptolemy XV (43-30 BC).

Caesar had nominated an heir and successor, his great-nephew, Gaius Octavius Thurinus (63 BC-AD14), who was also his adopted son. Octavius' real father, Gaius Octavius (100-59 BC) came from a respectable but undistinguished family; his maternal grandfather, however, had made a brilliant marriage to Caesar's sister, Julia. Antony was to slander the young man by claiming that Caesar had forced him to become his lover as the price of adoption; Antony's brother, Lucius, declared that the boy was so effeminate he softened the hairs on his legs by singeing them with red-hot walnut shells. At the time of Caesar's death, Octavius was a young man of nineteen, studying rhetoric and Greek literature in Apollonia on the Dalmatian coast. He was summoned home by his mother and, although the will had not yet been read, sailed back to Italy. When Octavius reached Rome, he found a hostile Antony, deeply resentful of the young man who owed everything to his famous name, and he refused to hand over Caesar's treasure. Octavian began to pay out Caesar's legacies with his own money, taking care to let everyone know what he was doing. He raised a private army and sought the approval of Cicero. Cicero was an avid Republican with no wish to see another Caesar seize power in Rome; but he was flattered by the young man's attentions and in any case saw him as a means of destroying Antony, whom he hated. Octavian, however, did not wish to destroy Antony: he wanted to be recognised as his equal and given Antony's help in securing his position.

Sixteen months after Octavius arrived in Rome, Antony and Lepidus joined him in forming the Second Triumvirate, with the aim of pursuing and defeating Caesar's assassins. They needed money for this: and they obtained it by reintroducing the proscriptions first used by Sulla in the eighties BC as a means of obtaining for the state the property of men found guilty of crimes. In an orgy of proscriptions and sordid murders, the property of one hundred senators and some two thousand rich men was confiscated. The most notable victim

CHAPTER FOUR

CLEOPATRA AND ANTONY

Marcus Antonius, better known today as Mark Antony, was born in 83 BC into a distinguished Roman family. His grandfather, also named Antony, had been a leading public speaker until he was condemned to death by the seven-time Consul, Gaius Marius (*c.*157-86 BC), for his support for Sulla (see page 48), Marius' great rival. In 110 BC, Marius married Julia (*c.*130-69 BC), who was nearly thirty years younger than he and an aunt of Julius Caesar. Plutarch claimed that it was only by marrying a patrician woman that Marius was able to launch his political career. Julia was noted for her virtue and for the devotion she showed to her husband and their only son; and when she died, her nephew gave the funerary eulogy.

Mark Antony's father, Marcus Antonius Creticus, 'of Crete' (*c.*103-71 BC) did not play an important part in public life and was killed on a military expedition against pirates when Antony was twelve years old. Plutarch observed that he was a worthy, good man, not very rich but noted for his generosity - a trait that was later to be seen in his son. His wife, Julia Antonia (104-39 BC), was another lady from the Caesar family: she was a cousin of Julius Caesar. She bore her husband three sons, Marcus, Gaius and Lucius. After M. Antonius Creticus died in 71 BC, Julia married Publius Cornelius Lentulus, who, in 63 BC, allied himself with Catiline in a conspiracy to kill rivals in the Senate and burn Rome. The conspiracy was unsuccessful and Lentulus was executed on the orders of Cicero, thus initiating a lifelong hatred of Cicero on the part of Mark Antony, a hatred that ultimately proved fatal for Cicero, as described at the end of the previous chapter.

Julia Antonia became responsible for her sons' education, one that was appropriate for boys of their class. Antony was trained for a career in politics; his studies, therefore, concentrated on public speaking and logic. Plutarch states that Antony grew up to be a very beautiful youth, but, sadly, fell under the influence of Gaius Scribonius Curio, a partisan of Julius Caesar, who led him into a life of drinking and dissipation that resulted in a huge amount of debt - six million sesterces. He then became a follower of Clodius, who had infamously gatecrashed the Bona Dea celebrations (see page 55), and who, according to Plutarch, was the most insolent and outrageous demagogue of the time. Antony quickly realised that he needed to disassociate himself from Clodius; but he had set a pattern of behaviour that he followed for the rest of his life. He was sometimes lazy, impatient with detail, occasionally reckless, overfond of carousing, gambling and women. He was also, however, brave and athletic, loyal to his friends and adored by his soldiers.

In 58 BC, the twenty-five-year-old Antony went to Greece to complete his education, as was the tradition with many young men of his class. He studied grammar and rhetoric in Rhodes and Athens, where he met Aulus Gabinius, the governor of Syria between 57 and 55 BC, and went on to serve as a cavalry commander under Gabinius in campaigns in Judea and Egypt, a somewhat surprising career development since he had had no military training. However, he did come from a prominent family and his mother was well connected; it could even be that Uncle Julius had had a hand in the appointment. Antony himself might have realised that time was passing and he needed to make his mark on the world.

When Ptolemy XII Auletes solicited Gabinius to restore him to the throne of Egypt, Gabinius was at first reluctant, in spite of a proffered bribe of ten thousand talents. Egypt was, after all, a sovereign state, and the jurisdiction of his governorship ended at the Syrian border. Antony persuaded him to undertake the task; and was ordered to march overland with the cavalry to Pelusium. He captured the city, rendering the way safe for Gabinius to follow with the army. When Auletes entered Pelusium, he gave orders for its citizens to be put to the sword: Antony prevented the slaughter, an action that gained him a great reputation in Alexandria and the army as a merciful and gallant soldier. Antony's magnanimity in victory was not to be emulated by Auletes: according to Dion Cassius, he ordered many of the most illustrious (and rich) citizens to be put to death 'as he needed much money' - presumably to pay the ten-thousand-talents bribe. During Antony's time in Alexandria after Auletes had been restored to the throne, Cleopatra was fourteen years old. It is improbable that the two spoke to each other, but the young princess may have seen this tall, muscular young man, with his thick, curly hair and the physique of a gladiator; and doubtless she had heard stories about the gallant twenty-eight-year-old soldier and filed them away in her memory.

After the Egyptian campaign, Antony chose not to return to Rome but instead sailed to Massilia (Marseilles) and then made his way to Gaul to join his uncle, Julius Caesar. Antony's military career in Gaul was a successful one. In 52 BC he was made quaestor, which in this case meant quartermaster general, and a year later was left in command of fifteen cohorts in northern Gaul. Antony returned to Rome in 50 BC, when his friend Curio, thanks to his own eloquence and to the money supplied by Julius Caesar, contrived to have him made first a tribune and then an augur. Tribunes were expected to represent the interests of the common people against those of the aristocratic members of the Senate; crucially, they had the power to veto unfavourable Senate decisions. An augur was responsible for observing and interpreting omens such as lightning during storms, or the flight of birds, for guidance in public affairs. Antony took this religious position seriously: he was to keep it for many years.

Antony became tribune at a critical time: Caesar chose it as the starting point for *Commentarii de Bello Civili* (Commentaries on the Civil War), his own account of his war against Pompey and the Senate. In 49 BC, the Senate determined to bring Caesar to book for what they claimed was his abuse of power. They proposed to pass a decree that Caesar disband his army and return to Rome. Antony and his fellow tribune, Quintus Cassius, vetoed the motion and were ejected from the Senate, an unprecedented move that was illegal in that it deprived the people of Rome of their

Senatorial representation. Claiming to be in fear for their lives, Antony and Cassius disguised themselves as servants and set off north in a hired carriage to join Caesar. The actions of the Senate gave Caesar the excuse to march on Rome, stating that he was doing so in defence of the people's representatives – the tribunes – against the illegal action that had been perpetrated against them. Cicero was to claim later, in his Philippics, that Antony was as much the cause of the civil war that followed as Helen was of the Trojan. Plutarch disagreed: in his opinion, Caesar was not so feeble as to be so carried away by the sight of two tribunes in a hired carriage that he would declare war on his own country; this was a decision that he had made long before.

In the civil war that ensued, Antony was given several important military assignments and distinguished himself. In 49 BC, he was left in charge of the troops that remained in Italy; the following year, he was in command of the army's left wing at the battle of Pharsalus. During Caesar's sojourn in Egypt, Antony was appointed his second-in-command in Rome; and when Caesar became Dictator in 44 BC, Antony became his Master of Horse. According to Plutarch, Antony endeared himself to his soldiers, training with them, living with them for long stretches at a time, and giving them as many presents as he could afford. However, he was not so popular with other people. Again according to Plutarch, he was too lazy to pay attention to people who came to him with complaints and listened impatiently to petitions. He undoubtedly preferred to be a man of action, not just on the battlefield but also in the bedroom, for he had a reputation for over-familiarity with other men's wives.

Antony was to have four, possibly five, wives of his own, most of them married for money or for political advantage. His first wife was Fadia, daughter of Quintus Faius Gallus. This was a marriage that should not have taken place since Fadia was only the daughter of a freedman whilst Antony was an aristocrat. However, Fadia's father was a *rich* freedman and Antony always needed money. The only Roman source attesting to the marriage is Cicero, who mentions it in his Philippics and in a letter (Number 16) that he wrote to his friend, Atticus. Cicero says that Fadia and her children were all dead by 44 BC at the latest, presumably, in view of Antony's later marriages, long since divorced, for a Roman man was only allowed one wife at a time. Cicero, a bitter enemy of Antony, could of course have been making the claim that Antony had been married to a lower class woman to blacken his reputation. In his late twenties, in furtherance of his career, Antony married his cousin Antonia Hybrida Minor. She bore him a daughter, Antonia, and they remained married for about eight years. He divorced her in 47 BC, accusing her of adultery with Publius Cornelius Dolabella, the husband of Cicero's daughter, Tullia.

Almost immediately after divorcing Antonia, Antony married Fulvia (*c.* 83-40 BC), a formidable woman who was to play a significant, if brief, role in the political struggles and chaos that followed the assassination of Julius Caesar. She was more or less the same age as Antony and, like him, had been married twice before. Fulvia was a provincial, having been born in Tarentum in Apulia, the daughter of Marcus Fulvius Bambalio, a rich plebian: she was his only child and therefore heiress to a huge fortune. Her first marriage, some time before 58 BC, had been to a patrician, Publius Clodius Pulcher (*c.*93-52 BC), who, as tribune, was extremely popular with the Populares, although Plutarch dismissed him as a demagogue. She bore him a son, also named Publius Clodius Pulcher, and a daughter, Clodia Pulchra, who years later was to be married off to Octavian. Four years before his marriage, Clodius had gained notoriety through his actions at the Bona Dea festival. His alibi that he was not in Rome on the day of the festival was refuted in court by Cicero, marking the beginning of a bitter enmity between the two men.

In 52 BC, Clodius ran for political office in competition with a rival, Titus Annius Milo, and after the campaign escalated into violence, Clodius was killed by Milo and his followers. Fulvia entered history after her husband's murder, lamenting in public over his dead body and displaying the wounds he had received at the hands of his assassins, an act that stirred up anger against Milo. The body of Clodius was taken to the Forum, where it was cremated. In the trial that followed, Fulvia's testimony moved those in court to tears; and in spite of Cicero's defence of Milo, he was exiled to Massilia (Marseilles), although not for long. The deceased Clodius had had control of many gangs; after his death they transferred their allegiance to Fulvia, giving her power and status. As Clodius' widow and mother of his children, she was also a symbol and a reminder of him, and was able to transfer this power to her future husbands.

Once the customary mourning period of ten months was over, Fulvia contracted another advantageous marriage, this time to Gaius Scribonius Curio. His background was less distinguished than that of Clodius, since he was a member of a newly risen consular family, but he may have been even richer than Fulvia's late husband. A year after his marriage, he won election for the post of tribune and Fulvia was pregnant with his son. In 49 BC, Curio was killed while fighting for Julius Caesar in North Africa against the army of King Juba I of Numidia. His death left Fulvia a very eligible widow. She was rich, she had proven herself fertile, she had links with Clodius' political organization; and her husband would be stepfather to Clodius' children, strengthening his position. She enjoyed her widowhood for several years before marrying for the third, and last, time. She had known Mark Antony for many years, since he was a good friend of both her husbands; and in 46 BC, she married him. In spite of her being in her late thirties, they were to have two sons together: Marcus Antonius Antyllus and Jullus Antonius.

It is not clear to what extent Fulvia was the driving force behind the careers of her first two husbands but Plutarch insisted that she was the dominant partner in her marriage to Antony. The Roman historian, Marcus Velleius Paterculus (*c.*19 BC - AD 31), stated that she had nothing of the woman in her except her sex: he, however, was biased in favour of Octavian and was denigrating Fulvia in order to belittle Antony. Presumably accounts of Fulvia's ghastly treatment of Cicero's tongue (see page 72) were designed to show her acting in an unwomanly, unseemly, way; but it is possible to have a certain amount of sympathy for her actions: Cicero had long been an enemy of her husband, and therefore of her, and had mounted several vicious personal attacks on Fulvia herself.

From the outset, Fulvia promoted Antony's interests, so much so that she became the target of public abuse, more than any other Roman noblewoman had ever experienced. She profited from the proscriptions that followed the formation of the Second Triumvirate in 43 BC and greatly enriched herself, as did Antony, with both of them gaining immense power. Fulvia's fame reached Phrygia (in central Turkey), where the city of Eugenia was renamed Fulvia in her honour. She was on the verge of becoming the most influential woman in Rome thanks to the marriage of her twelve-year-old daughter, Clodia, to Octavian. Her hopes were dashed in a most insulting manner when the bridegroom sent his wife back to her mother with a letter saying that he was returning her in the same condition as the one she had been in before the marriage, in other words, the marriage had not been consummated.

The members of the Second Triumvirate had allotted to themselves different parts of the Roman Empire. Lepidus, the most ineffectual and least trusted member, was assigned Africa where the other two considered he could do little or no harm. Octavian was allotted Italy, Spain and Cisalpine Gaul. Antony, who was the real victor of Philippi, was given Macedonia, Greece, and the East, the term that was applied to Bythinia, an area of north-western Asia Minor in what is now Turkey, other regions of Asia Minor, Syria and Cyrene. Egypt was still regarded as an independent kingdom. He was also given the rest of Gaul, which provided him with twenty-four legions, all under the command of men who were loyal to him. Confident that they would defend his interests in that area, Antony turned his attention to the East, which he knew was the richest part of the Roman Empire. His grand plan was to make the countries of the East into one unit, possibly with the inclusion of Egypt, and to use its wealth to fund his legions in a war against Parthia.

In 42 BC, Antony left Octavian in Rome, wearing himself out coping with war and seditions, and began a journey to the East purportedly to raise the wherewithal to fulfil Julius Caesar's promise that every common soldier should receive a payment of five thousand drachmas. He stayed in Greece for a time. He liked Athens and gave the city many gifts, but soon made his way into Asia Minor, where kings vied for his attention by competing for the honour of who would present him with the most valuable presents. They knew that Antony was there to wring as much money from their countries as he could: this he duly did, imposing punishing levels of taxation. Unlike Julius Caesar, Antony gave no thought for the morrow; he lived for the day and took no steps to establish solid foundations. With no immediate war to distract him, Antony fell back into his old ways, indulging in wine, women and song. According to Plutarch, lute-players like Anaxenor, flute-players like Xuthus, dancers like Metrodorus, and a gaggle of other local entertainers flooded into Antony's quarters where they outdid the Italian parasites there in their effrontery. When Antony arrived in Ephesus, he was met by women dressed as female devotees of Dionysus, the Maenads, whose name means 'mad' or 'demented', driven so by their consumption of the wine of which Dionysus was god. In their songs, Antony was greeted as Neos Dionysus, the New Dionysus, ironically an epithet by which Cleopatra's father had chosen to be known.

In the late summer of 41 BC, Antony travelled to Tarsus (south-central Turkey), 20 km (12 miles) inland from the

Mediterranean and built on the banks of the river Cydnus. There, he decided that a meeting with Cleopatra would be advantageous. He must have met her several times when she was living in Rome, and probably realised that she was no ordinary woman but a capable politician who had not just been the mistress of Julius Caesar but had gained the respect of the great man. Her advice on the situation in Asia Minor and the East could prove invaluable; and besides, she was the ruler of an immensely rich country. Accordingly, he despatched one of his commanders, Quintus Dellius, with a letter for Cleopatra in which he commanded her to come to Tarsus and answer the accusation that she had given assistance to Cassius before Philippi. Plutarch claimed that when Dellius saw Cleopatra's face and heard the subtlety in her speech, he was convinced that Antony would never harm her but favour her above all others. He advised Cleopatra to go to meet Antony dressed in her best finery and without fear of him since he was the gentlest and kindest of soldiers. Cleopatra was not reluctant to meet this gentle and kind soldier; she had great confidence in her own charms: they had drawn Julius Caesar to her and might prove even more effective with Antony. When she first met Caesar she had been a young, inexperienced girl, she was now a mature, twenty-eight-year-old woman in the prime of life.

Cleopatra did not hurry to Tarsus. She set about assembling money and gifts that reflected the affluence of her country. She had no intention of arriving before Antony as a supplicant: she was, after all, a queen, descended from a long line of kings, whilst he was a commoner, even if he was the most powerful man in the Roman Empire. She had a capital city that was superior to Rome in its palaces and public building and, especially, in its administrative structure: compared with Alexandria, Rome was provincial. Cleopatra knew Antony's reputation as a lover of excess and voluptuousness; and took these aspects of his character into consideration when she made plans for her arrival in Tarsus. At last, she came sailing up the river Cydnus in a barge that, whilst smaller than the vessel in which she had taken Julius Caesar on his Nile cruise, surpassed it in splendour. Plutarch described the barge as having a gilded stern and outspread sails of purple, with oars made of silver. Shakespeare gave a more memorable description in *Antony and Cleopatra*:

The barge she sat in, like a burnished throne,
Burned on the water; the poop was beaten gold;
Purple the sails, and so perfumed that
The winds were love-sick with them; the oars were silver,
Which to the tune of flutes kept stroke, and made
The water which they beat to follow faster,
As amorous of their strokes. For her own person
It beggared all description: she did lie
In her pavilion - cloth-of-gold of tissue -
O'er picturing that Venus where we see
The fancy out-work nature: on each side her
Stood pretty dimpled boys, like smiling Cupids,
With divers-coloured fans, whose wind did seem
To glow the delicate cheeks which they did cool,
And what they undid did.[1]

Plutarch described how perfumes from the barge wafted across the water to the banks of the river, which were thronged with people who had either followed the vessel from the Cydnus delta or rushed out of the city to see it. Antony awaited Cleopatra's arrival seated on a raised platform, the tribunal, in the market place, expecting the queen to come ashore to greet him. She had no intention of doing so. Antony sent a message inviting her to dine with him; but she declined and invited him to come to her, an astute move since it meant that their first meeting would be on what was, technically, Egyptian soil. Antony, willing to show courtesy and good humour, accepted. He was deeply impressed by the magnificence of the preparations that had been made to receive him and his officers, particularly the number of lights resting in branches that were let down, some in squares, some in circles, so that, as Plutarch claimed, the whole thing was a spectacle that had seldom been equalled for beauty.

The next day, Antony repeated his invitation to dinner, and this time it was accepted. He would have liked to outdo Cleopatra's party in splendour but, realising the impossibility of this, he was the first to mock his own rustic ways. His tastes were simple, like those of any ordinary soldier: he was happy if he had access to quantities of wine, an ample supply of good food, and women, lots of women. In contrast to Cleopatra's sharp, sophisticated wit, his was coarse and broad, more suited to drinking sessions with his comrades than conversing with a cultured woman: the queen, however, adapted herself to his manners; a clever move, for what man could resist such subtle flattery? If

Cleopatra's erudition, wit and elegant manners, not to mention her famously seductive voice, had attracted Caesar, they overwhelmed the bluff man's man, Antony. He was so captivated by her that in the autumn of 41 BC, he followed her to Alexandria, ignoring the fact that his legions were assembled in Mesopotamia, ready to enter Syria and begin the campaign against the Parthians.

In Alexandria, Antony gave himself up to a hedonistic lifestyle. He had fond memories of the Alexandria of his youth; on this visit he fell in love with the city. He 'went native', speaking in Greek rather than Latin and wearing a Greek tunic rather than a Roman toga. Plutarch claimed that he was like a boy on holiday; certainly he seemed to be without cares and enjoying the 'infinite variety' not only of Cleopatra but of the exotic, sophisticated entertainments that were on offer. When exactly Cleopatra became his mistress is not clear, but in view of the fact that she bore him twins some time in 40 BC, it probably happened shortly after their encounter in Tarsus. They formed a group known as 'The Society of the Inimitable Livers', whose members, declared Plutarch, took turns to entertain one another at a cost that was extravagant beyond belief. Cleopatra's self-indulgence is exemplified by the story of her destruction of a priceless pearl (see page 13). She bound Antony to her by matching his every mood; she was not only his lover, she was his friend and very liberal hostess; she drank with him, matching him cup for cup, she gambled with him and hunted with him; she looked on when he was exercising at arms, doubtless enjoying the sight of his gladiator's physique. At times, she even dressed herself as a servant-woman and accompanied him, also dressed in servant's clothes, on nocturnal rambles through the streets of Alexandria, making mischief by knocking on doors and windows and running away like mischievous children. These escapades were presumably more to Antony's taste than Cleopatra's; and the Alexandrians put up with them good-humouredly, saying that they were grateful that Antony reserved his tragic activities for Rome, keeping comedy for them.

Antony was so much in thrall to Cleopatra that she was able to convince him that her sister, Arsinoe, must be eliminated, something she had failed to persuade Julius Caesar to do. Caesar had instead sent her to live in Ephesus. She was now residing in the sanctuary of the great Temple of Diana, where she was treated with respect - she was, after all, the daughter of a king of Egypt and nominally the queen of Cyprus. The High Priest of the temple even addressed her as Your Majesty. It is possible that Arsinoe was plotting against Cleopatra; in any case, she was the last of her siblings and it must have seemed to Cleopatra that it was advisable to remove this potential threat. Accordingly, Antony sent soldiers to Ephesus where they killed Arsinoe on the steps of the sanctuary. Antony presented Cyprus to Cleopatra.

Cleopatra was not above playing tricks on her lover; as Plutarch related, she was with him on a fishing trip on which Antony was catching no fish. Not wishing to be seen as an unsuccessful angler, he ordered several local fishermen to dive underwater and put fish that they themselves had caught onto his hook. He then began to reel in fish so fast that

Cleopatra saw through his ruse. She said nothing but brought him back next day to fish again: this time, however, she had divers attach a salted fish to his hook. To much laughter, he drew up the fish that he had supposedly caught and Cleopatra advised him to leave fishing to 'we poor sovereigns of Pharos and Canopus'. Your game, she told him, 'is cities, provinces and kingdoms'.

Cities, provinces and kingdoms eventually reclaimed Antony's attention. In the spring of 40 BC, he received two messages: one that Fulvia and his brother, Lucius Antonius, had formed an alliance against Octavian and were at war with him; and the other that the Parthians had overrun Syria and had advanced as far as Lydia and Ionia in what is now Western Turkey. Antony was forced to leave Egypt to deal with the situation. Shortly after his departure the queen gave birth to twins whom she named Alexander the Sun (Helios) and Cleopatra the Moon (Selene). They were not to meet their father, and Cleopatra was not to see her lover, until nearly four years later. She was able to keep in touch with developments; and what she heard about Antony's actions must have made her despair of ever holding sway over him again.

After Antony's departure from Egypt, Cleopatra did not sit about moping. She had work to do. Her private fortune had become depleted, the Egyptian army and navy needed to be reconstructed. Fortunately, Egypt had begun to prosper again after her father's mismanagement, and she was able to accomplish these tasks. There was a great demand in Rome for works of art; Alexandria had long been famous for its handicrafts and was now exporting vast quantities of them. Local craftsmen were adept in cutting and engraving gemstones and metals, and made use of a variety of materials such as gold, silver, glass, crystal and even obsidian. The city was famous for its linen and glass industries, and for the manufacture of sail cloth and papyrus. Egypt as a whole produced vast quantities of grain; indeed, it was eventually to become known as the granary of Rome. Rome could not match the city for the study of astronomy and mathematics. Above all, Alexandria was the centre of Hellenistic culture.

During the winter of 41-40 BC, Lucius Antonius had been besieged in Perusia (present-day Perugia) and starved into surrender. The city was sacked, but Lucius Antonius was spared and given a command in Spain, after which he disappeared from history. Although Octavian blamed Fulvia for the insurrection, which may have been an attempt by her to attract Antony's attention and lure him away from Cleopatra, she was allowed to escape unharmed and flee to Greece, where she became sick and died in the Peloponnesian city of Sicyon. Octavian's propagandists claimed that it was her grief over Antony's extreme anger with her because of her meddling that was the cause of her death; and Antony certainly blamed himself for it, or at least for not having kept her ambitions in check.

Up to this point, Antony himself had no quarrel with Octavian, whom he dismissed as an inexperienced young man; but having learned that he was forgiving Julius Caesar's enemies and intriguing with Sextus Pompey (67-35 BC), the younger son of Pompey the Great, he sailed to Brundisium (modern Brindisi) in the autumn of 40 BC to demand an explanation from Octavian. The two men had now become jealous of and angry with each other, but they managed to reach an accommodation and renewed the terms of the Second Triumvirate: Antony was still in charge of the East, Octavian the West, and Lepidus remained in Africa. Four years later, Sextus Pompey was driven from his base in Sicily and escaped to Miletus in Asia Minor.

Fulvia's death had come at an opportune time, for it enabled Antony to cement his reconciliation with Octavian by the age-old means of marriage. His bride was Octavia (*c.* 69 BC-11 BC), sister of Octavian, both of them borne to Gaius Octavius (see page 70) by his second wife Atia Balba Caesonia, the niece of Julius Caesar. Octavia had been married to an early opponent of Julius Caesar, Gaius Marcellus, by whom she had had two daughters and a son. Only five months after the death of Marcellus, she was married to Mark Antony, by special dispensation of the Senate since it was within the ten-month mourning period. In September, 39 BC, she bore him a daughter, Antonia, later known as Antonia Major, who was to become the grandmother of the Emperor Nero.

In contrast to Fulvia, Octavia was a quiet, domesticated woman, regarded as the epitome of traditional Roman feminine virtues. She was an upholder of family life, something that Antony did not have much interest in, and respected throughout Rome for her noble behaviour, her loyalty and her humanity. She raised Antony's two sons alongside her own children; and in due course took on the responsibility for caring for the children of Cleopatra. In modern times, it might have been said about her that 'the woman is a saint'. After the tempestuousness of his previous two relationships, Antony probably thought of her as worthy but dull, although he must have realised that she was one of the few

had managed to do without her for the last several years. Antony was not a romantic, he was pragmatic: within months of leaving Cleopatra in Alexandria, pregnant, he had married Octavia, even though it was only for political reasons. But Cleopatra was still ambitious to establish a Romano-Ptolemaic dynasty that would rule the East; she knew that Antony needed Egypt as a base for his campaign against Parthia and Alexandria as a capital city in place of Rome. For the second time in her life, she went to meet Antony in Syria. And for the second time she did not come as a supplicant. Her offer of support came with conditions attached. During the first period of their liaison, Antony had been married to Fulvia. Cleopatra did not require him to divorce her. This time, she insisted on marriage. Antony knew that if he divorced Octavia any relationship between him and Octavian would be at an end, and so he hit upon the strategy of having the marriage performed according to Egyptian ritual, thus avoiding the charge of bigamy, which was an indictable offence under Roman law, and allowing Octavian to consider him still married to Octavia, since the legitimacy of the Egyptian marriage would not be recognised in Rome. Cleopatra considered an Egyptian ceremony to be perfectly acceptable, especially as Antony offered her a dowry consisting of large parts of both Syria (Coelesyria) and Cilicia (southern Turkey), Palestine, Phoenicia, except for Sidon and Tyre (cities on the Mediterranean coast of what is now the Lebanon), Arabia Nabatea (southern Jordan), and Jericho, although not the rest of Judea, which he left in the hands of its king. With the addition of Cyprus and Sinai, Egypt ruled an empire that was the largest it had been for a thousand years. Antony also made a gift to Cleopatra of the library of Pergamum (modern Bergama in Turkey), which reputedly contained 200,000 papyrus rolls and was second in importance only to the Great Library of Alexandria.

Antony intended that he should rule over the Egyptian empire with Cleopatra at his side. Knowing the Roman distaste for kings, he did not make Julius Caesar's mistake but chose to call himself 'Autocrator' or 'Ruler Absolute'. A new system of coin-dating was introduced; and from 37 BC, the heads of both Cleopatra and Antony appeared on the obverse and reverse sides of coins, she as Queen and he as Autocrator. In the spring of 36 BC, Antony set off for Mesopotamia with the intention of mounting a campaign against Parthia. Cleopatra went with him, seemingly with the intention of being at his side during the war. Although she was not entirely in favour of the undertaking, considering it risky and liable to cost her a great deal of money, the excitement appealed to her. At Zeugma, the major crossing point on the river Euphrates in south-eastern Turkey, she discovered that she was pregnant and, doubtless to Antony's great relief, decided to go back to Egypt so that she could give birth to the child in Alexandria. Rather than return home by sea, she took a circuitous land route via Damascus and along the river Jordan to Jericho so that she could visit her new possession. There she was met by the King of Judea, Herod (73-4 BC).

Herod's father had appointed him governor of Galilee in 47 BC. After Julius Caesar's assassination, he collaborated for a time with Cassius, one of the assassins, who had taken over Syria; but when Cassius was defeated at Philippi, Herod switched sides and became not only Antony's ally but also his friend. In 40 BC, Antony persuaded Octavian and the Senate to make Herod king of Judea, claiming that he was the man best suited to dealing with the Parthians who had invaded the country. Even with Roman help, it took Herod three years to expel the Parthians from Judea and Jerusalem, but at last he took Jerusalem, where he was welcomed by its inhabitants and earned their gratitude by trying to prevent the Romans from pillaging the city.

Herod came to meet Cleopatra with the intention of discussing Jericho, a strategically important city and one which Josephus described as a divine region. It enjoyed a tropical climate that produced quantities of palms, henna and balsam, the 'balm of Gilead', prized for its perfume and for its medicinal properties. Herod must have been annoyed that Antony had given this jewel in his crown to Cleopatra, but after some hard bargaining he persuaded her to rent it to him. Cleopatra also decided to lease the bitumen fields of Nabatea to Malichus, its ruler. Her interest in this area was finally to cost her dear when she persuaded Antony to launch Herod and his army against the Nabateans, thanks to which the Herodian forces were otherwise occupied when the Battle of Actium (see page 116 was fought, an absence that may have contributed to Octavian's victory.

Herod and Cleopatra distrusted each other: he saw her as a threat and feared that one day she would persuade Antony to hand over his kingdom to her. According to Josephus, Cleopatra toyed with the idea of seducing Herod. He, claiming that the lustful Egyptian queen was making eyes at him, determined to have her killed before she left his territory. Of course, Josephus was writing nearly a hundred years after the event, and was being careful not to alienate his Emperor, Vespasian, by deviating from the traditional Roman vilification of Cleopatra. In any case, it is highly improbable that she would risk her relationship with Antony, the Autocrator, for the sake of a brief affair with the ruler of a petty kingdom, no matter how charming he was reputed to be - at least until the Slaughter of the Innocents. Cleopatra, contrary to Roman claims, was not a slave to her lusts; and besides, she was in the early months of pregnancy.

Herod escorted the Queen as far as Pelusium and from there she journeyed to Alexandria to await the birth of her baby. Tradition has it that Cleopatra brought back from Jericho cuttings of the prized balsam shrubs and had them planted in the ancient Egyptian city of Heliopolis (near modern-day Cairo). In the autumn of 36 BC, she gave birth to her fourth child, a boy whom she named Ptolemy Philadelphus, or 'Brother-loving', a sentiment not often observed in the Ptolemaic dynasty. At this point, Cleopatra was probably expecting a rosy future. Once Antony had conquered the Parthians, avenging Crassus' defeat at Carrhae and restoring Roman honour, his popularity in Rome would know no bounds and he would be able to oust Octavian from political life. It would no longer be necessary for Antony to maintain his marriage to Octavia; Cleopatra would be recognised as his wife in Roman eyes and together they would rule over a vast empire.

Meanwhile, Antony had started his campaign against Parthia. The traditional route into the country taken by his predecessors had been across the desert from the west; but Antony intended to lead his army on a long detour round to the north and take the Parthians by surprise by coming at them from an unexpected direction. He had assembled a huge army of about one hundred thousand men, supplemented by a large number of siege engines, including a battering ram that was over 24 metres (80 feet) long. His plan of campaign was a good one, but handling such a large army needed a great deal of organisation and attention to detail, and Antony, who prided himself on being a man of action, was never much given to petty-fogging matters of detail. Besides, it was difficult to keep the movements of such a large army secret.

A better general than Antony - Julius Caesar, for example - would have made sure that the faster speed of travel of the army was adapted to the slower pace of the siege engines, which would be necessary for the capture of cities, and to that of the supply trains, which were vital to keeping the army fed and watered. More successful generals than Antony demonstrate patience: Antony had always shown himself to be impatient. He decided to press ahead with his troops, leaving the siege engines and the supply trains behind, and hasten towards his first major target, the city of Phraaspa, in Media (north-west Iran), believed to house not only the treasury but also the wives and family of the king of Media - a target that brings to mind the capture of the wives and family of the Persian king, Darius III, by Alexander the Great. Antony was confident that his name and the size of his army would induce the city to surrender; but he was mistaken. Even worse, he received news that his supplementary forces had been attacked by the Parthians and all the siege engines had either been captured or destroyed. The besiegers lost heart and Antony was forced to take ruthless measures to enforce discipline by means of decimation, that is, the

Roman military practice of dividing mutinous soldiers into groups of ten, each group drawing lots to choose one of their number, who was then bludgeoned to death by the others.

Winter was approaching and it would not be long before snow blocked the mountain passes. Reluctantly, Antony decided to raise the siege and, low on supplies, begin the arduous journey out of Media. This journey has sometimes been likened to Napoleon's retreat from Moscow, during which he was defeated by 'General Winter'. Both retreats were terrible experiences. The Parthians harried Antony's army, their archers picking off hundreds of men. The ranks were further thinned by starvation and disease. It was to Antony's credit that he ate the same rations as his men, and displayed conspicuous valour. Plutarch opined that although Antony's preparations for his Parthian campaign struck terror into hearts even as far away as India, they came to nothing because Antony was in too much of a hurry to get back to Cleopatra, a ridiculous claim since Antony was well aware of the importance of a victory over the Parthians, and besides, he was not a man to consider a campaign well lost for love.

Even Plutarch had to concede that as a leader Antony was held in great respect by his soldiers: it was such that 'their obedience and goodwill and the degree to which every man of them - whether good or bad, officers or private soldiers - chose honour and favour from Antony rather than life and safety, was something that even their forefathers could not have surpassed.' Plutarch also noted that 'by the way in which he shared in [their] distress and difficulties, he made even the wounded and the sick as eager to serve him as those who were well and strong.'

Finally, after a month of terrible privation, the army reached Armenia, a friendly territory. A review of the troops was carried out and it was reckoned that some twenty-four thousand men had perished, mostly on the retreat. The losses did not end there: on the trek through the snow-bound Armenia, a further eight thousand were lost. Finally, Antony and the remains of his army reached Syria, and set up camp to the north of Sidon. They had reached safety and, importantly, had not lost the legionary eagles, those symbols of Roman pride. Antony had managed to hold his army together by the strength of his personality, but having reached safety he lost his customary optimism and sought solace in wine. Messages had already been sent to Cleopatra and later that year she arrived in person with food and clothing for the army, and money, although not as much as Antony had hoped for. Funds would have to be extorted from the countries he 'owned' by even more onerous taxation.

Cleopatra must have been shocked at Antony's condition. She persuaded him to come back to Alexandria with her to recuperate: and it is from this time on that Cleopatra gained the ascendancy over her husband. In Alexandria they proceeded to lead a more sober life than the one they had enjoyed during Antony's first sojourn there. There were no more frivolous escapades, no revival of the Society of the Inimitable Livers. Cleopatra attempted to persuade her husband that his obsession with Parthia would lead nowhere; and that his real enemy was Octavian. During Antony's absence from Rome, his rival had achieved great success. He had persuaded Lepidus to retire from public life, leaving his province in Africa in Octavian's hands; and in 35 BC, Sextus

Pompey had finally been caught and executed without trial by the general, Marcus Titius, whose life he had once spared. The execution was not popular with the Romans, who had a fondness for Sextus Pompey for his opposition to the Second Triumvirate. Octavian escaped opprobrium by claiming that Titius had acted on Antony's orders.

Octavian was master of the West: it seemed certain that he would one day soon attempt to make himself master of the East also. First, however, he held out an olive branch to Antony. He had statues of his fellow triumvir erected in the Forum, and granted him the right, hitherto restricted to Octavian alone, to dine with his wife and family in the Temple of Concord - the wife in question, of course, not being Cleopatra. These honours were an invitation to Antony to take up his place in Roman society again, and to be united with his wife, Octavia. Antony spurned them: he had no intention of leaving Cleopatra or of giving up his position of Autocrator.

Antony may perhaps have heeded Cleopatra's advice to forget his ambitions in Parthia, but in 35 BC, the King of Pontus, who had been taken prisoner by the King of Media during Antony's Parthian campaign, arrived unexpectedly in Alexandria. He had been sent to Antony with the news that Media's alliance with Parthia had come to an end, and with an invitation from the King of Media to Antony to come and help him defeat the Parthians. Antony could not resist: a victory against the Parthians would ensure his popularity with the Romans and raise him to the status of hero and would be certain to earn him the Triumph in Rome that he yearned for. It was at this point that the wily Octavian sent Octavia to Athens with gifts and money for Antony and his officers, a large quantity of clothing for his army and two thousand men selected from the praetorian guard. The two thousand soldiers were nowhere near the numbers needed to replace those lost in the recent Parthian campaign: they were, in effect, a bodyguard for Octavia, although, even so, they were a thousand men fewer than had been thought necessary to escort Fulvia to Greece.

Antony sent a letter to Octavia in which he informed her that he was in Syria busy preparing for a new campaign against Parthia and instructing her to stay in Athens and await his arrival. Cleopatra did not dare let him go: it would have been risky to allow him to see Octavia again in case he remembered that in Roman eyes she was his one true wife - and that she was a very agreeable one, calm and restful in contrast to the more tempestuous Cleopatra. Antony was nearly fifty years old, exhausted by his Parthian campaign: the danger of him falling into the comforting arms of Octavia was a real one. Plutarch claimed that Cleopatra pretended to be dying of love for Antony, refusing to eat and making doe-eyes at him whenever he came near her, appearing to swoon whenever he left her. She often allowed him to see her surreptitiously wiping away tears as if she did not want him to see her cry. Such behaviour from Cleopatra must have taken Antony by surprise; she was not known to be a weepy, clinging women, quite the opposite. Antony, in his turn, was not known for his understanding of feminine behaviour, and was uncomfortable with displays of womanly emotion. However, he was a warmhearted man and so he gave in to Cleopatra's wishes. He allowed himself to be taken back to Alexandria.

Octavia returned to Rome, where Octavian instructed her to leave her husband's house and come to live with him. Upper class Roman women of the time normally did what their male relatives, especially those who were heads of their families, told them to do; but Octavia was allowed to refuse Octavian's invitation and stayed in Antony's house looking after the children and facilitating meetings between her brother and Antony's friends. She even begged her brother to ignore Antony's treatment of her, insisting that it should not be used as an excuse to go to war with each other. According to Plutarch, her conduct was inadvertently damaging Antony since he now became hated for wronging such a fine woman. That the damage was inadvertent is doubtful: Octavian knew that the contrast between his noble sister's exemplary behaviour and Antony's desertion of her in order to live with a strumpet foreign queen was harming Antony in the eyes of many Romans. That strumpet foreign queen was well aware that Antony's public insult to Octavia would inevitably lead to war between West and East.

Antony spent the winter of 35-34 BC in Alexandria, as was customary; but in the spring he moved his headquarters to Syria. He sent a message to the Armenian king, Artavastes II, inviting him to come to Syria to discuss a second campaign against Parthia. The invitation was declined; and Antony marched into Armenia, took Artavastes II prisoner and declared that from thenceforth Armenia was to be a Roman province. Antony's army pillaged the country and seized a vast amount of loot, including a solid gold statue of the goddess, Anaitis, which was taken from her temple and broken into pieces, which were distributed amongst the troops. Antony then returned to Syria and began negotiations with Artavastes I, the King of Media. The six-year-old son of Antony and Cleopatra, Alexander Helios, had been betrothed to the King of Armenia's daughter. That alliance was, of course, no longer possible, which left the boy free to marry the Median princess, Iotapa, a much more advantageous alliance since the King of Media consented to the boy and his bride being named as heirs to the throne of Media, a step towards Antony's ambition of founding dynasties of his own flesh and blood in foreign lands. Rome was informed that a new province had been added to the Empire, a fact that did not overly impress the people of Rome since they had little interest in places far distant from Rome. They did, however, look forward to Antony's arrival in Rome to celebrate his triumph over Armenia with the customary lavish entertainments, games and banquets in which they could join.

Antony, however, did not return to Rome; instead, in October, 34 BC, he arrived back in Alexandria and began preparations for a Triumph. This was unheard of: Triumphs were a Roman institution, awarded by the Senate only after close scrutiny of the conduct and outcome of a successful campaign. A Triumph was the highest honour that the Roman state could confer upon a general. It was certainly not an honour that a general could award himself. That Antony not only did so but exacerbated the situation by proposing to hold the Triumph in Alexandria was a serious political error, perhaps the greatest he ever made. Unlike Cleopatra, he was not an astute politician. His actions not only insulted the Roman Senate and the people of Rome, they alienated the population by depriving them of the free feasting and entertainments that were customarily theirs on such occasions. It may be that Antony decided to celebrate a Triumph in Alexandria because he realised that Octavian would block attempts to award him a Triumph in Rome, especially since the victory in Armenia was not as impressive as a successful campaign against Parthia would have been. It seems clear that Cleopatra made no attempt to dissuade Antony from committing this reckless provocation. She must have realised that it would signal a break between Antony and Rome, transforming him from a noble Roman to an oriental potentate, and a recognition of her as Antony's true wife. She surely hoped that the Alexandrian Triumph would be a step along the road that would eventually lead to Rome losing its standing as the capital of the Empire and being replaced by Alexandria, something that had always been her ambition.

The Triumph that Antony celebrated in Alexandria was more spectacular than any event the city had ever witnessed. A troop of Roman soldiers led the way, their shields decorated with a large letter C, shockingly inferring that these legionaries owed their allegiance to Cleopatra rather than to Rome, or even to Antony. Behind them came units of the Egyptian army followed by representatives of Rome's allies and client states. They were followed by Armenian prisoners at the head of whom walked King Artavastes, in golden chains, and his wife and children. They were followed by cartloads of looted Armenian treasure and captured insignia, behind which came representatives of captured cities, each bearing a golden crown destined to be worn by Antony. Lastly came

Antony himself, resplendent on a chariot. He was not dressed as a Roman general but as the god Dionysus - he had, after all, been greeted as Neos Dionysus on his arrival in Ephesus eight years previously. This was a Triumph being celebrated for the Hellenistic peoples of the East and of Alexandria and, to a lesser extent, for the people of Egypt beyond the capital city. It was not a celebration for Rome, which probably took it as a signal that Antony had finally deserted it.

The Triumphal procession made its way to the Temple of Serapis, the Serapeum (see page 27), where Cleopatra awaited him, dressed as the goddess Isis and seated on a golden throne, flanked by the priests of Serapis. Once there, Antony made sacrifices to the god in thanks for his victory, an action that seems reasonable since Serapis was the tutelary deity of the city in which the Triumph was being held but which was interpreted by Antony's enemies as a deliberate insult to Rome, whose own protector god, Jupiter, was the customary recipient of Triumphal sacrifices. One of those sacrifices had traditionally been the captive ruler whose country had been conquered; and Artavastes must have prepared himself to meet the same fate as Vercingetorix. Antony may have realised that to put to death a cultivated man such as Artavastes, a recognised poet and playwright, would have been a gratuitous act of cruelty, and he was never a cruel man. So Artavastes was spared, presumably with Cleopatra's agreement, in spite of the fact that he had refused to kneel before her in homage and had instead greeted her by name.

Once Serapis had been accorded his dues, the Triumphal procession wended its way to the Gymnasium, a significant choice of venue since it was near the tomb of Alexander the

Great. Along with city and army dignitaries, a large crowd of Alexandrians had been gathered to witness proceedings. Antony and Cleopatra took their places on golden thrones set on a silver platform; below them, seated on their own thrones, sat Caesarion, Alexander Helios and Cleopatra Selene. Antony then proceeded to read out his will: in a division of the Egyptian Empire, Cleopatra and Caesarion were to be co-rulers of Egypt, Cyprus and Coelesyria; Alexander Helios was given Armenia and Media, and Parthia when it had been conquered; and the baby, Ptolemy Philadelphus, was given Phoenicia and Cilicia. In spite of the example of her mother being a queen regnant, Cleopatra Selene was not appointed a ruler but was given Libya and Cyrenaica as a dowry. Caesarion was only thirteen years old at the time, Alexander Helios six, and Ptolemy Philadelphus less than two, so it would be some time before they would be able to exercise their kingships.

Antony's sons were dressed for the Triumph in clothing appropriate to the countries they were to govern, Alexander Helios in Persian costume, the baby Philadelphus in Macedonian, complete with Macedonian-style boots and the cap encircled by a diadem that was worn by Macedonian rulers. The choice of costume for Philadelphus was making a political point: although Macedonia was a Roman province, one day it would have a king, and that king would be a Ptolemy claiming the land of his ancestors. Caesarion was presumably attired in Roman or Greek style, but as far as he was concerned, the political point was made by the title he was given - 'King of Kings' - an indication that Antony was keeping faith with his friend Julius Caesar by promoting the interests of his son above those of his own children. He was also sending the message that although Octavian had been named in Caesar's will as his adopted son and successor, it was Caesarion who was of Caesar's own flesh and blood and therefore the rightful heir of his father. Coins were struck to commemorate the Armenian Triumph. Surviving coins show the head of Antony wearing the Armenian crown on one side, with the simple inscription 'Antoni Armenia Devicta' (For Antony, Armenia having been vanquished). The head of Cleopatra appears on the other side, and the inscription 'Cleopatrai Reginae Regum Filiorum Regum' (For Cleopatra, Queen of kings and of the children of kings).

Antony was quick to acquaint Octavian with the dispositions he had made regarding the Eastern Empire. Octavian was astounded at his rival's presumption. In law, Antony ruled over the Eastern Empire with Rome's permission; its territories were not his to parcel out among his children. Octavian had the contents of Antony's letters to him made public so that everyone could see how vaunting Antony's ambitions were. Not only had he proclaimed himself a King, in defiance of Rome's detestation of such an office but he had publicly recognised Cleopatra as his wife, in spite of still being married to Octavia, and appointed Cleopatra's sons, including Caesarion, the 'so-called son of Julius Caesar', as Octavian put it, as kings.

Cleopatra must have been delighted with events. Not only was she Queen of Egypt, with the master of half of the Roman Empire at her side, her territorial rule had been expanded and her children appointed kings over large areas of the East; and since they were minors it was, of course, Cleopatra herself who ruled in their name. She may have had high hopes that one day soon, Caesarion would be recognised as his father's true heir and rise to power in Rome. Whether Antony had thought of all these new arrangements for the Eastern Empire by himself is doubtful. He was not known for his skill in statecraft. In all probability, it is Cleopatra who should be given the credit for them. Antony was ambitious, certainly, but perhaps needed Cleopatra to stiffen his backbone, with the result that he sent messages to Rome inviting the Senate to ratify his actions. He also offered to give up his position as triumvir if Octavian would do likewise. Octavian, naturally, had no intention of ceasing to be a triumvir, or of recognising Antony's apportioning of the Eastern Empire, known in Rome as 'The Donations'. In the annual debate in the Senate on 'The State of the Republic', held in 33 BC, he escalated his rivalry with Antony by openly criticising him for his conduct. A copy of Antony's will, as was customary, had been deposited with the Vestal Virgins in Rome; Octavian had it published in order to drum up feelings against Antony, knowing that the contents would appal the citizens of Rome. In this he was correct; and the Senate was so shocked that it outlawed Antony. Octavian allowed his rival's relatives and friends to leave Rome and join Antony, an astute move since it prevented a fifth column subverting Octavian in Rome during the war that was inevitably approaching. Within months, he had declared war, not upon Antony, even if he had been declared an outlaw, but on Cleopatra. The real cause of the war was Antony's recognition of her son, Caesarion, as

Caesar's heir: Octavian needed to rid himself of this threat to his own position.

The Romans who chose to join Antony included two recently appointed Consuls, Gnaeus Domitius Ahenobarbus and Gaius Sosius and over three hundred of the one thousand Senators who made up Rome's ruling body. The defections allowed Antony to claim that the Senate in Rome was invalid, and he set up a senate of his own, not in Egypt but at Ephesus, famous as the first and greatest metropolis in Asia Minor. The city boasted the Temple of Artemis, a building made of white marble, cypress and cedarwood, ornamented with gold, and with Ionic columns over eighteen metres (sixty feet) high. It was regarded as one of the Seven Wonders of the ancient world, and in Egyptian eyes took its place alongside two of their own Wonders, the pyramids at Giza and the Pharos of Alexandria. The goddess to whom the temple was dedicated had a special resonance with Cleopatra. Artemis was idealised by Greek men as a virgin huntress but Greek women prayed to her to protect them during childbirth; her fame at Ephesus was due to the fact that there she merged with an ancient Anatolian mother-goddess. The Romans identified Artemis with Diana, their own divine huntress, and Diana in her turn was identified with Venus, the goddess of beauty, love and fertility with whom Cleopatra was closely associated.

Ephesus was never wholly Greek as a city, still less Roman, but one with a strong Anatolian ethos. Its great temple offered banking services and kings and commoners from over a wide area were happy to entrust it with their treasure. Trade made the city prosperous: Ephesus lay on the western coast of what is now Turkey, at the mouth of the River Cayster overlooking the Aegean Sea towards Athens, just over 300 km (199 miles) away. It boasted a fine harbour used by dozens of ships from Greece, Egypt, Sicily, Spain and the Black Sea each day. Antony and Cleopatra chose Ephesus as the assembly point for their forces and those of their allies, and Ephesus became the largest naval and military centre in the world. Eight hundred fighting ships were assembled by Antony, and Cleopatra brought from Egypt two hundred warships and thousands of sailors, soldiers and supporting workmen, as well as munitions and military equipment, clothing, and, above all, a vast amount of grain, food and money, enough to supply the whole army, according to Plutarch, for the whole of the war. The rulers of Mauritania, Upper Cilicia, Cappadocia, Paphlagonia, Thrace, Galatia and many others answered Antony's call to arms. One ally and friend of Antony did not put in an appearance, Herod of Judea, who was busy conducting a campaign of his own against the Nabateans. As things turned out, Herod was wise to be otherwise occupied: the ultimate victor, Octavian, allowed him to keep Judea as a reward for his absence.

Cleopatra was very much in evidence at her husband's side, playing an active part in the preparations for war. The Senators and Consuls who joined Antony in Ephesus were unpleasantly surprised to see that Cleopatra was behaving as if she were already Queen of Italy: she had replaced her household guards with Roman legionaries whose shields were inscribed with her name, and she called army headquarters 'the palace' and spoke of Antony as her commander-in-chief. Whenever she moved outside 'the palace' she reclined on a litter carried by eunuchs; if Antony was in attendance, he walked deferentially several steps behind. Gnaeus Domitius Ahenobarbus, in particular, was offended by Cleopatra's actions. A descendant of an old Roman family and an ardent republican, he refused to address Cleopatra by her title but only by her name. He urged Antony to send her back to Alexandria lest she alienate his allies. Cleopatra sought help from Publius Canidius, Antony's most important general. According to Plutarch, Canidius pointed out to Antony that the Egyptian fleet would fight more willingly in the presence of their queen, and Egyptian money would be more readily available if it was thought that Cleopatra herself was in need of it. He went on to ask which of the kings who had joined the expedition was superior to her in wisdom, for she had for a long time governed a vast kingdom, alone. Canidius clinched his argument by reminding Antony that Cleopatra had learned from him how to handle great affairs (no pun intended). Cleopatra stayed. Disgusted, many of Antony's soldiers offered the command of the army to Ahenobarbus. He did not think it honourable to accept their offer but instead did an arguably more dishonourable thing by defecting to Octavian. The ever magnanimous Antony, not a man to bear a grudge, sent his departing friend's equipment after him; but a short time later, Ahenobarbus, who had been suffering from a fever when he defected, died.

In the spring of 32 BC, Antony and Cleopatra decided to spend the summer on the island of Samos, which lay only a short distance away from Ephesus. Samos was a rich and powerful city-state, known for its vineyards and wine production, particularly the famous Samian wine.

It had been the birthplace of several renowned scholars, notably the sixth-century BC mathematician Pythagoras; the fourth-century BC astronomer, Aristarchus, the first man to postulate that the earth revolves round the sun; and the fourth-century BC philosopher, Epicurus, who held that the highest good came from freedom from pain and the pursuit of pleasure. Why Antony and Cleopatra considered a holiday in Samos a suitable preparation for war is unclear; but a period of rest and recuperation as Epicureans possibly held a certain attraction, especially for Antony. In contrast, 'pretty nearly the whole world' was, according to Plutarch, filled with groans and lamentations, fearful of the coming war. As predicted by Ahenobarbus, Antony's deference towards Cleopatra had alienated many of the men who had followed him to Ephesus, and one by one, they began to slip away. This did not prevent the Queen and her consort tempting fate by holding festivities in celebration of what they were sure was their forthcoming victory over Octavian.

Once summer was over, Antony sailed away from Samos, seemingly with a vague intention of attacking Italy. Off Corcyra (Corfu), however, he received news that enemy ships had been sighted in the Adriatic and changed course for Athens, where he set up residence with Cleopatra. She was determined to outdo her rival, Octavia, in popularity with the Athenians and began to cultivate the city's leading citizens. Antony arranged for a statue of the Egyptian queen in the guise of Isis to be erected next to his own on the Acropolis; and began to replicate the hedonistic lifestyle he had enjoyed in Samos and Ephesus. He was now fifty-one and a life of hard campaigning, drunkenness and debauchery had taken its toll. He was no longer the young soldier who had fought so successfully at Philippi; he had become irresolute, unable to make up his mind. The life that he was living with Cleopatra had begun to shock people. She, apparently, did not care. She did, however, care that Antony was still married to Octavia. Cleopatra did not intend to arrive in Rome, once her confidently expected victory had been achieved, merely as Antony's mistress in Roman eyes: the Romans must recognise her as his wife. The usually impetuous Antony had delayed a divorce from Octavia, partly, perhaps, in order to avoid humiliating this decent woman, but mainly because he wished to avoid the final breach with his brother-in-law that such a divorce would precipitate, until he was ready to go to war.

For once in her life, Cleopatra's political judgement deserted her and she persuaded Antony that this was the moment to announce that he had divorced his wife, Octavia. Octavian chose to react to the news with an offer to Antony of a safe passage to Italy to discuss their differences. Antony seems to have been tempted by the offer, weary as he was in mind and body. Cleopatra was not, and so he hesitated. He must have realised that Cleopatra, whom Romans considered to be an evil woman who had used her black arts to enslave two of their most famous generals, would be unwelcome on Roman soil. Indeed, her appearance in Italy would be worth several legions to Octavian. Several of his friends pointed out to him that his treatment of Octavia, that paragon of a dutiful Roman matron, would have alienated her many admirers; and among his own supporters it would be seen as confirmation that he was totally subservient to Cleopatra. A panicked

Antony addressed his legions, promising them that within two months of victory he would restore the Republic.

Cleopatra was not amused. She could see that the original reason for the war, to oust Octavian and put her son, Caesarion, in his place, was being subverted into a quest to restore the Republic and foster notions of liberty and democracy that were alien to her autocratic nature. Like Macbeth, Antony was 'infirm of purpose'; like Lady Macbeth, she would have to 'screw [his] courage to the sticking-place'.[3] At this time, Cleopatra, who seemingly carried her thirty-eight years lightly, was undoubtedly in the ascendancy over the prematurely aged Antony. Many stories were circulated about his behaviour: it must be supposed that not all of them were untrue. It was said that he once got up from his couch at a banquet and demeaned himself in front of the guests by rubbing the Queen's feet, a duty that was normally performed by a slave; and that if he received a note from the Queen whilst he was conducting official business he would call a halt to the proceedings so that he could read it. Cleopatra's enemies claimed that she kept Antony in a state of besotted servitude by means of magic potions. In reality, he had become a maudlin, uxorious alcoholic.

While Antony and Cleopatra were dallying on Samos, Octavian was experiencing difficulties in Italy. A rebellious population feared that war with Antony would result in crippling taxes for them and that the inevitable interruption in food supplies would soon lead to starvation. If Antony had invaded Italy in 32 BC, he most probably would have defeated Octavian: but he decided to let Octavian bring the war to him. He was not expecting to have to fight a big battle on land and decided to leave four of his legions in Egypt, four in Cyrene and three in Syria. He had about 100,000 foot soldiers and twelve thousand cavalry with him in Greece; Octavian had the same number of cavalry but only eighty thousand foot soldiers. But Antony had wasted time and was about to lose the initiative.

Before Cleopatra could re-motivate Antony, news came that Octavian was massing troops and ships at Brundisium (modern Brindisi), a city on the south-east coast of Italy overlooking the Adriatic Sea. Towards the end of 32 BC, Antony and Cleopatra set up winter quarters at Patras on the western coast of Greece at the entrance to the Gulf of Corinth and some 400 km (250 miles) across the sea from Brundisium. Unwisely, they sent the fleet up to the Ambracian Gulf. The Gulf, which is about 8 km (5 miles) wide, penetrates the land for about 16 km (10 miles). It seemingly made a good shelter, but in winter it was cold and suffered from heavy rainfall. Antony, with an inattention to detail that he often displayed, neglected to ensure that supply lines were maintained, and gradually, supplies ran out and the ships' crews began to fall ill and die: by the end of the winter it is estimated that a third of them had been lost. Antony was forced to press into service untrained local men - farmers, ploughmen, donkey boys, even travellers passing through the area - to form a set of motley crews. It has to be remembered that Antony was a general not an admiral. Octavian was not an admiral, either, but he did have the wisdom to put his fleet in the charge of a man who had achieved considerable success at sea against Sextus Pompey, the brilliant Marcus Vipsanius Agrippa (*c.*63-12 BC).

At the end of the winter of 31 BC, Octavian struck. He dispatched a fleet of ships under the command of Agrippa to take the Greek port of Methone in the southwest Peloponnese. This meant that Agrippa was able to capture ships coming from Egypt with supplies for Antony. Whilst Antony was preoccupied by what he thought was probably an advance guard for a major assault to his south, Octavian had left Brundisium with his army and landed at Epirus to Antony's north, cutting off the troops that Antony had stationed at Corcyra. The rivals were in no hurry to bring matters to a climax. Antony waited, trying to prepare his troops for a land battle against Octavian. His position was being weakened by the almost daily desertions of his allies: he needed to act decisively, knowing that he was best suited to a battle on land rather than one at sea. Octavian, however, refused to be drawn into a land battle.

Antony had no choice but to fight Octavian at sea. Cleopatra, of course, was blamed for this fateful decision. According to Plutarch, 'her opinion that the war should be decided with ships prevailed.' Antony and Cleopatra were not in the best of positions: their ships had lain at anchor for months in warm waters and must have been considerably fouled by barnacles and algae; the timbers of many of them may have been infested with *Teredo navalis,* or naval shipworm, a mollusc that bores into ships' timbers. In contrast, Agrippa's ships had doubtless been hauled ashore in the winter months to have their hulls scraped and their timbers caulked. As the saying goes, 'Lying in harbour rots ships and rots men.'

The fleets of Antony, Cleopatra and Agrippa met each other in a great sea battle fought on 2 September, 31 BC, off the

Ionian coast of Greece at Actium. Antony's ships were formed into three squadrons, parallel to the shore and rather close to it. They made up the front line. A fourth squadron, consisting of sixty ships under the command of Cleopatra herself, took up position in the rear as reserve. Ominously, her ships had been laden with her private plate, jewellery and treasure. They were also laden with their masts, sails and rigging, as were Antony's ships. Sea battles were not fought under sail, they were fought by banks of oarsmen driving the rams on the prows of their vessels into the enemy ships, followed up by fighting men leaping on board the opposing vessels. That the ships were equipped for a sea voyage, indicating that Antony was prepared for failure and flight, must have demoralised the members of his fleet.

Soon after noon on 2 September, a fresh breeze sprang up, something that was known to happen in the Ambracian Gulf at that time of year. Plutarch makes express reference to this phenomenon, writing that since a wind was blowing off the sea, Antony's men became impatient for battle, knowing that the strength of the wind would increase as the day wore on, making it difficult for them to make headway against it. He goes on to explain that in the battle there was no ramming or charging by one ship against another because Antony's great vessels were incapable of the speed that would make such an action possible; and the enemy vessels were wary of attacking the sides of Antony's ships, which were constructed of huge timbers that would have shattered their rams. The battle, therefore, resembled one being fought on land, or rather, as Plutarch states, a struggle around a fortified town. There were always three or four of

Octavian's vessels around each one of Antony's, which were defending themselves with catapults against the enemy's spears and missiles.

While the battle was still underway, its outcome not yet decided, Cleopatra's squadron made sail, charged through the centre of both lines, and made off. Antony boarded a light craft and, according to Shakespeare, 'like a doting mallard', followed her. Cleopatra's enemies were only too eager to blame her for the subsequent loss of the battle. Dion Cassius wrote that she was tortured by suspense and fearful of the outcome, whichever way it went. In a remark that managed to be both sexist and racist he claimed that her actions were due to her nature as a woman and as an Egyptian. There is another explanation for her action. She did not turn tail and run in a cowardly fashion, her ships charged bravely through the middle of the enemy lines. This may have been a plan of action prearranged with Antony and was in fact a bid to disrupt the battle. Under oars her ships were too heavy for ramming; under sail, in a strong wind, every Egyptian ship had a chance to damage, if not sink, an enemy vessel. The ploy failed, and once to leeward of the battle, Cleopatra's fleet could not manoeuvre round to re-engage. Antony, for his part, intended to live to fight another day, and meant his fleet to break off battle and follow him. This they were unable to do because they were surrounded by enemy ships; and they continued to fight heroically until the next day. Antony had never fought a sea battle in his life, and it is perhaps unlikely that he had conceived a plan of action that involved a constructive manoeuvre by Cleopatra. It seems probable that he had expected to lose the battle at Actium, greatly outnumbered as he was, and that his main concern was that he and Cleopatra should escape unharmed.

Plutarch wrote that Antony caught up with Cleopatra's flagship and was taken on board. He made no move to see the Queen but went forward into the bows and sat there, alone, with his head in his hands, giving himself up to despair. Several days later, the ships reached the southernmost tip of the Peloponnese and dropped anchor. Cleopatra's serving women, including Charmion and Iras, at last persuaded Antony to come to the Queen's cabin and take something to eat. While they were making ready for the voyage back to Egypt, the terrible news reached them that Antony's fleet had indeed been defeated and all the ships either burned or captured. The optimistic, ebullient Antony of old might have told himself that he could build another fleet; and that he still had his army. But that Antony was long gone. In any case, his despair was deepened by the news that his army, which had been left under the command of Publius Canidius, had surrendered to Octavian. It had been demoralised by the news that Antony had not been killed in battle but had escaped with his foreign queen leaving them to their fate. It was not difficult for Octavian to win them over, especially when he promised them that once the war was ended, they would receive the same amount of land as would be distributed among his own veterans.

Canidius and Antony's senior commanders realised that Octavian would show them no mercy and fled under cover of darkness to join Antony. Not wishing that men who had loyally supported him over the years should suffer for doing so, he generously selected a transport ship laden with a great deal of money as well as gold and silver objects from the royal treasury, and told them to divide the contents of the ship between themselves. In tears, they refused to accept the gift; and he sent them to Corinth for their own safety with instructions to his steward there to look after them and keep them hidden until they could make peace with Octavian. Canidius made his way to Egypt where, in 30 BC, he was charged with desertion and executed on Octavian's orders.

Antony and Cleopatra arrived back in Egypt, landing at Paraetonium (modern Mersa Matruh), some 240 km (150 miles) west of Alexandria. The Queen sailed straight away to Alexandria in order to arrive there before word reached the city of the defeat at Actium so that she could make sure that she was in full control of affairs. At the end of September, 31 BC, she sailed into the Great Harbour at Alexandria, her ship bedecked as though in celebration of victory. By this time her natural resilience had begun to reassert itself. Antony remained in Paraetonium, understandably reluctant to face the possibility of the crowds coming out into the streets to mock him for his failure, unwilling to meet the pitying stares of his friends and courtiers in the palace. Instead, he stayed with two companions in Paraetonium.

His choice of companions is interesting. One was a Greek rhetorician named Aristocrates. Antony had studied rhetoric in his youth. The other was a Roman, a soldier named Lucilius, who had fought alongside Brutus at Philippi and had impersonated Brutus to allow him to escape once it was clear that the battle was about to be lost. Lucilius was captured; and was forgiven by Antony for the deception, a magnanimous act that earned Antony Lucilius' loyalty for the rest of his days. Antony spent weeks in Paraetonium, contemplating suicide but unable to summon up the willpower to kill himself. At last, he was persuaded by his two companions to return to Alexandria and to Cleopatra.

Once in Alexandria, Antony took himself off to a rocky promontory, determined to be a recluse. Cleopatra coaxed him back to the palace where she tried to tease him out of his melancholy and urged him to drink and be merry, not, this time, as a member of The Society of Inimitable Livers but as a member of a circle she named 'the Diers Together'.

Cleopatra had not been idle during Antony's absence from her side. She must have realised by now that her husband's mental and physical faculties had waned considerably. He was never going to be co-ruler of the whole Roman Empire with her; indeed, if Octavian decided to add Egypt to his conquests, she herself would be in danger of losing her throne. She set about consolidating her own governance of the East. Her son, Alexander Helios, had been betrothed to the King of Media's daughter for three years and the young Median princess was now living in the royal palace in Alexandria. Artavastes, the deposed king of Armenia, was also living in Alexandria - but in a prison. Cleopatra could be reasonably certain that once the victorious Octavian arrived on the scene, he would seize Media, and would probably not only restore Artavastes to his throne, but hand over Media to him as well, thus cancelling the arrangements Antony and Cleopatra had made for gaining a throne for their son. Cleopatra decided to remove Artavastes from the scene and thwart any plans that Octavian may have for him. She ordered him to be put to death and sent his head to the King of Media as a token of her good faith.

Cleopatra had long ago begun to plan her Monument, the place where her body would lie after her death. It was not constructed near the Sema (see page 25) and the royal necropolis, which were near the Great Library, but on the edge of the sea on the eastern side of the Lochias Promontory, near the Temple of Isis/Aphrodite. The site for Cleopatra's Monument was carefully chosen: she identified herself with Isis, and presumably intended that worshippers coming to the Temple to make offerings to the goddess would also make offerings to Cleopatra. The Monument was large and noted for the quality of the workmanship that had gone into the construction of its chambers. It was a two-storey building, which was probably largely constructed from marble and cedarwood. The main chamber on the ground floor contained the great stone coffin, the sarcophagus, in which the Queen's body would rest. For the ancient Egyptians, a tomb was one's House of Eternity (*per nekhekh*) and a temple was the House of the God (*per neter*): for Cleopatra, it was fitting that her body should be placed in the house of god for eternity.

Cleopatra planned to use her Monument as a refuge should Octavian reach Alexandria. Accordingly, she had vast amounts of treasure taken to it - gold, silver, ebony, ivory; her jewellery; cinnamon - and piled onto a heap of firewood covered with bitumen-soaked rope. It was her intention to set fire to her treasure rather than let it fall into Octavian's hands. She herself had no intention of living to walk in Octavian's Triumph and determined to die by her own hand. According to Plutarch, she collected all sorts of deadly poisons and tested them on prisoners to see which of them caused the least painful death; and observed that fast-acting poisons made death the most painful. Luckily for the prisoners, it is not very likely that Cleopatra actually needed to experiment with poisons since the ancient Egyptians had long been famous for their pharmaceutical knowledge and the Ptolemies had been known to poison their enemies. She did have experiments carried out using venomous animals and decided that the bite of a hooded cobra, often called an asp, was the gentlest way to die since it induced unconsciousness very quickly without any spasms of pain and with only a little perspiration on the face. A person who died from the bite of an asp looked as though they were sleeping serenely but could not be aroused from that sleep.

Meanwhile, in a desperate effort to come to an accommodation with Octavian, she sent him emissaries bearing gifts and a proposal that she should abdicate in favour of Caesarion and her sons by Antony. Antony also made overtures to Octavian, suggesting, over-optimistically, that he should retire into private life and live out the rest of his days in Egypt or, if that were deemed not possible, in Athens. Octavian did not deign to answer Antony's request, but he kept Cleopatra's gifts and sent her evasive replies. He knew about the vast amount of treasure piled up in her Monument and was eager to lay his hands on it; he needed it to pay his soldiers. He therefore decided not to risk Cleopatra behaving precipitously but sent her messages promising that she would be well treated as long as she expelled Antony from Egypt or, even better, had him executed. This demand had a damaging effect on Antony's morale, as Octavian knew it would, and made him distrustful of Cleopatra. It is impossible to know how tempted she was by Octavian's offer, but she must have realised that Octavian would never consider himself safe as long as she and Antony lived. It is extremely unlikely that Octavian had any other intention than to invade Egypt, capture both the country and its Queen, and take her back to Rome to walk in chains at his Triumph and to be executed in the traditional way at its climax.

Caesarion also was in danger: although Octavian had always insisted in public that the young man was not Julius Caesar's son, in his own mind he suspected that he was. Caesarion would always be a threat to him. Accordingly he made arrangements to have him killed. Cleopatra had sent her son away from Alexandria intending that he should sail up the Nile to Coptos (modern Qift, 43 km/25 miles north of Luxor) and then travel across the desert to Berenice, on the Red Sea, there to await developments. Since Berenice was a major centre for trade with Arabia and India, there was a chance that if things went badly he could escape to India. Sadly, Roman forces caught up with him, and it is said that the young man was strangled by a Roman officer. By the time Caesarion met his death his mother was also dead: Cleopatra never knew the fate of her favourite child, the one person in her life to whom she gave her love unconditionally.

In May, 30 BC, Octavian arrived in Syria with legions from Asia Minor. Since Herod of Judaea had already deserted his erstwhile friend, Antony, the way to Egypt was unimpeded. Octavian ordered his general, Cornelius Gallus, to attack Paraetonium in the west whilst he himself advanced on Pelusium in the east. Octavian later claimed that he took

Pelusium by storm, although Plutarch and Dio Cassius, ever eager to traduce Cleopatra, both claimed that she treacherously ordered the city to surrender without a fight. Gallus captured Paraetonium. On 1 August, 30 BC, Antony ordered the fleet moored in the Great Harbour of Alexandria to set sail for Pelusium to attack Octavian's ships that were mounting a blockade a few miles away. The fleet was visible to Antony on shore and as he watched he saw the men rowing his ships lift their oars out of the water, a signal to the enemy that they did not intend to attack. At almost the same time, Antony's cavalry deserted him and rode off to join Octavian. Realising that the situation was hopeless, Antony's troops broke ranks and retreated into Alexandria. It was reported that Antony cried out that Cleopatra, for whom he was fighting, had betrayed him - the words of a despairing, bitter man, which show Antony's unwillingness to blame himself for his failures.

When Cleopatra heard the news of Antony's defeat, she summoned her two favourite serving women, Iras and Charmion, and with them made her way to her Monument. Once inside, the women bolted the great entrance door and took up residence on the upper floor. According to Plutarch, a message was sent to Antony informing him that Cleopatra had committed suicide, perhaps to encourage him to do the same out of shame lest it be said that a woman had had more courage than a Roman general. Even so, he did not intend to kill himself; instead, he turned to his faithful slave, Eros, from whom he had earlier extracted a promise that, if the time ever came, Eros would kill him. Eros took the sword out of Antony's scabbard, but, unable to bring himself to use it on his master, stabbed himself. Antony took up the weapon and thrust it into his body under the ribs. He intended it to pierce his heart, but in what might be described as a final act of incompetence, he stabbed himself in the stomach, condemning himself to a long, painful death. When news of Antony's condition was sent to Cleopatra in her Monument, she gave orders to her secretary, Diomedes, to bring Antony to her.

The simplest way for Antony to be carried in to the Monument would have been through the front door. Possibly Cleopatra thought it unwise to risk opening it in case unwanted visitors crowded in. So, according to Plutarch, the Queen and her two servants hoisted Antony up into the Monument through an upper floor window by means of ropes. Antony was a heavy man and, almost literally, a dead weight, unable to assist in the process. However, the women managed to haul him up. It is possible that they were aided by men perched on ladders, especially since Plutarch recounts the story of what happened next as though he had read eyewitnesses accounts of it - the eyewitnesses being the men on ladders peering through the window through which Antony had been admitted. He recounts that Cleopatra abandoned herself to grief, beating and scratching her breasts, smearing Antony's blood on her face, and calling him her lord, her husband, her emperor. The dying man rallied sufficiently to beg her to come to terms with Octavian; and recommending Proculeius, one of Octavian's advisors, as a man she could trust in negotiations. Then, Plutarch writes, Antony begged her to rejoice with him in remembering the good times they had shared in the past. Antony told her: 'I have been among the most powerful and illustrious of men, and now I am not ignobly conquered but a Roman by a Roman overthrown.'

All very true, but a remarkable speech by a man on the point of death; one suspects Plutarch of a little embroidery. On 10 August, 30 BC, Antony died in Cleopatra's arms; and she was left to contemplate what was sure to be a short future.

When Octavian received notification of Antony's demise, he decided that it would be appropriate if he reacted to it in the way that Julius Caesar had greeted news of Pompey's death: with tears. He waited for what he considered to be a suitable length of time, and then summoned several of his friends to his tent. It was not sufficient that he had defeated his rival, he felt the need to destroy his reputation by reading out copies of letters that he, Octavian, had sent to Antony. It was clear from these letters, he claimed, that he had always tried to achieve a reconciliation between them, only to be met with arrogance and insults. No doubt he implied that this was all because Antony was in thrall to that ambitious foreign woman.

Meanwhile, Proculeius (see above) had made his way to the Monument, and, standing outside its massive door, called out to Cleopatra to admit him. She refused and would only talk to him through the firmly closed door. He tried to reassure her that she could trust Octavian to treat her well; she knew very well that he would not: it was she, not Antony, against whom Octavian had declared war; it was she who had been branded as the enemy of Rome. Octavian now sent his general, Gallus, to talk to the Queen. He kept her distracted while Proculeius and two officers entered the Monument at the rear, probably climbing up the same ladders that had been used by the men who had helped Cleopatra and her serving women hoist Antony up into the Monument. They entered by the window through which Antony had been dragged and saw him lying there in the room before them. They hurriedly ran down the stairs and rushed towards Cleopatra, who took a dagger from her belt, meaning to kill herself. Proculeius wrested it from her. Cleopatra, Iras and Charmion were searched to make sure that they had not hidden poison with which to kill themselves, and taken to the upper chamber. Antony's body was removed and the Queen and her servants were left, closely guarded, to await Octavian's pleasure.

Octavian entered Alexandria at sunset. Before his arrival, he had given orders that there was to be no looting; and he took pains to present himself as a reasonable man. He went straight to the Gymnasium to address the great and the good of Alexandria who had been assembled there. He assured them that he did not hold them in any way responsible for the recent war; and that he greatly valued their wonderful city, partly because of its association with the great Alexander, partly because of its grandeur and beauty, and partly for its fostering of philosophy and the arts, of which he was a devoted admirer. A devotion to philosophy and the arts did not manifest itself in the orders he gave as soon as he reached the palace. Soldiers were sent to catch up with Caesarion and kill him. On being told by the treacherous tutor of Antony's eldest son, Antyllus, that the boy had taken refuge in the temple that Cleopatra had erected to Julius Caesar, he gave orders that he also should be killed. Antyllus was dragged from the altar to which he clung - an act of sacrilege - and once out of the temple, beheaded. His tutor stole a valuable gem that Antyllus had worn around his neck. Unluckily for him the theft was discovered and Octavian ordered that he be crucified. He was not the last person to die in that manner: during his reign, Octavian was to have so many people crucified, tortured or killed in other ways that he was named The Executioner, by his enemies at least.

Octavian then decided that a show of magnanimity was called for. Accordingly, he gave Cleopatra leave to bury Antony. She, and other female members of her court accompanied Antony on his last journey. He was buried in the tomb that had been built for him beside her Monument. Cleopatra did not mourn in a dignified, controlled fashion; instead she demonstrated her grief in the traditional Egyptian way by casting dust on her head, scratching her cheeks, tearing her clothes and wailing aloud, just as Egyptian women do today. She beat her breasts so hard that they became inflamed and she became feverish. Octavian permitted her to return to the palace.

A short time later, Cleopatra's physician, Olympus, informed Octavian that the Queen was feeling better. Octavian decided to visit her unannounced so that she would have no time to prepare herself. His visit to her chamber was recorded by Olympus, and it is his account of the last hours of Cleopatra's life that Plutarch read decades later. The encounter between the two enemies was probably the first time that they had seen each other, for Octavian was not in Rome when Cleopatra was there with Julius Caesar. The first glimpse of this woman who had been his *bête noire* could not have impressed him. She lay upon a pallet-bed wearing only a shift and sprang up as he came into the room to throw herself at his feet. Her face was disfigured, her hair tousled. Her eyes were sunken into

Right: 1. Philip of Macedon. (Louvre Museum, Paris)

Below left: 2. Olympias. (Louvre Museum, Paris)

Below right: 3. Alexander the Great depicted on a coin wearing the ram's horn of Zeus-Ammon.

Above left: 4. Ptolemy I Soter. (Louvre Museum, Paris)

Above right: 5. Cleopatra. (British Museum)

Left: 6. Octavian – bronze head from Meroe in modern Sudan. (British Museum)

Above left: 7. Juba II of Mauretania. (Musée Archeologie de Rabat, Morocco)

Above right: 8. Pompey's pillar, Alexandria. Wrongly attributed but one of the few surviving monuments.

9. Fort Qait-Bey, Alexandria – site where the Pharos or Lighthouse once stood.

Above: 10. Apis Bull in bronze. (Gulbenkian Museum, Lisbon)

Left: 11. Nefertiti – painted limestone bust. (Neues Museum, Berlin)

Opposite, top left: 12. Nefertiti – limestone statuette. (Neues Museum, Berlin)

Opposite, top right: 13. Nefertiti – quartzite head. (Egyptian Museum, Cairo)

Opposite, bottom: 14. Temple of Hathor, Denderah – exterior of main hall.

15. Temple of Hathor, Denderah
– interior of main hall showing
Hathor-headed column capitals.

16. Temple of Hathor, Denderah
– west side.

17. Temple of Hathor, Denderah
– showing on extreme right
and left reliefs of Cleopatra and
Caesarion.

18. Temple of Hathor, Denderah – relief of Hathor suckling Ihy, accompanied by Harsomtus.

19. Temple of Hathor, Denderah – the Iseum or Temple of Isis.

20. Temple of Isis, Philae.

21. Temple of Isis, Philae – David Roberts lithograph, 1834.

Above: 22. Temple of Horus, Edfu.

Right: 23. Temple of Horus, Edfu – main gateway, west wing, with relief of Ptolemy XII, father of Cleopatra, smiting his enemies.

24. Site of the Pergamon library in Anatolia, said to house somthing like 200,000 volumes according to Plutarch.

25. Actium, location of Antony's defeat at sea.

26. Relief from Abydos Temple of Seti I showing Maat (left) and Re, with obelisk between them.

27. Temple of Amun at Karnak – obelisk of Tuthmose I (1520–1492).

Left: 28. Osiris – bronze statuette.
(Hermitage Museum, St Petersburg)

Above: 29. Statuette of Isis suckling Horus.
(Hermitage Museum, St Petersburg)

Right: 30. Granite statue of Horus as a falcon at the Temple of Horus, Edfu.

Below: 31. Nekhbet (vulture) and Wadjet (cobra) as the uraeus on funerary mask of Tutankhamun. (Egyptian Museum, Cairo)

32. Wadjet (left) and Nekhbet (right) in human form, wearing crowns of Lower and Upper Egypt. Relief from exterior wall of main building in the Temple of Horus, Edfu.

33. Lillie Langtry (1853–1929) as Cleopatra.

Above: 34. American silent movie star Theda Bara (1885–1955) as Cleopatra. Only 20 seconds of the 1917 film still exist.

Right: 35. Evelyn Laye (1900–1996) as Cleopatra. She played the role on the London stage in 1925.

Above: 36. Claudette Colbert as Cleopatra, with Henry Wilcox as Antony, in Cecil B. DeMille's 1934 epic.

Left: 37. Vivien Leigh as Cleopatra in the 1945 British film adaptation of George Bernard Shaw's *Caesar and Cleopatra.* Rank lost millions on the film.

her face and her voice trembled. He raised her to her feet and told her to return to her bed.

Despite everything, according to Plutarch's version of Olympus' report, her famous charm and striking beauty had not entirely left her. Later Roman stories about the encounter claim that Cleopatra tried to seduce Octavian, but these are probably inaccurate. Instead, she seems to have decided to appeal to his sentimental side, if indeed he had one, and showed him letters that his uncle had written to her when she was young and beautiful and an ally of the Roman people. She pointed out to him that it was Julius Caesar who had himself placed the crown of Egypt upon her head. Octavian merely glanced at the letters, they were of no interest to him. Cleopatra's survival was - at least for the time being: he was determined that she should live long enough to be taken back to Rome to walk in chains in his Triumph. He therefore gave her assurances that his only concern was for her well-being: and she pretended to believe him.

When Cleopatra asked for permission to visit Antony's burial site, Octavian graciously granted her request, doubtless because doing so cast him in a favourable light. Cleopatra laid flowers on the grave and made sure that the soldiers who had escorted her heard her final words to her dead husband so that they could report them to Octavian. She told Antony that there would be no more flowers and libations from the captive Cleopatra for he, a Roman, would lie in Egypt, but she, an Egyptian, would be buried in Italy - a clear indication to Octavian that she was resigned to her fate as a sacrificial victim at the end of his Triumph. The soldiers escorting her, perhaps moved by her situation, allowed her to go to her Monument rather than back to the palace.

On 12 August, 30 BC, Charmion and Iras arrayed their Queen in her robes of state, with the crown she always wore as the manifestation on earth of the goddess, Isis. Accounts of her end tell of how a peasant arrived, ostensibly with a basket of figs as a gift for the Queen, and was allowed to enter the Monument. In the presence of Cleopatra and her two faithful maid servants, he revealed what was under the figs: two asps. Cleopatra wrote a letter to Octavian requesting that she be buried next to Antony and sent everybody, apart from Charmion and Iras, out of the room. She laid herself down on a golden couch and bared her breast to the asp.

As soon as Octavian received Cleopatra's letter, he realised that she was intending to commit suicide. He sent several of his officers hastening to the Monument in an effort to forestall her, but they arrived too late. They found the Queen lying dead, with the dead Iras lying across her feet and a dying Charmion attempting to adjust the Queen's headdress. There was no sign of an asp. It was said later that two bites were visible on Cleopatra's body, one on her breast and one on her arm. It was not apparent how Charmion and Iras had died, but presumably it was by swallowing poison. If Cleopatra did indeed die by means of a cobra's bite, then Wadjet, the cobra goddess whose duty was to safeguard the royal wearer of the uraeus,[4] had failed in her duty to protect the last and greatest ruler of the Ptolemaic Dynasty. She passed into legend, often traduced as a scheming harlot, especially by those Romans who could never forgive her for ensnaring two of their greatest citizens. The truth is quite different: Julius

Caesar and Mark Antony, those two great Romans, could simply have used Cleopatra as the Queen of what was then the richest country in the world to further their ambitions. The fact that Cleopatra 'managed' them so successfully was not because she was a harlot but an intelligent, well-educated woman whose political ability was the equal of theirs. Octavian was generous enough to have her buried alongside Antony. Neither grave has ever been found.

Postscript

Octavian Caesar, known after January 27 BC as Augustus (the revered one), the first Emperor of Rome, took Egypt as his personal estate and forbade any member of senatorial rank to set foot in it without his direct permission. He sent Cleopatra's three children by Antony - Alexander Helios, Cleopatra Selene, and Ptolemy Philadelphus - to Rome. The three children, the twins aged ten and their brother aged six, were paraded in Octavian's Triumph, the chains in which they were bound so heavy that they could scarcely walk. After their ordeal, they were taken into the household of Octavia, their father's former wife, to be brought up under her charge.

Augustus was confident enough to disregard the tradition that entitlement to the Egyptian throne passed through the female line, which meant that whoever became the husband of Cleopatra Selene had a claim to be ruler of Egypt. He arranged for her to be married to the Numidian prince, Juba (*c.* 52 BC-AD 23), a Berber from North Africa. He was the only child and heir of King Juba I of Numidia, who had been an ally of Pompey, and who, in 46 BC, had been defeated by Julius Caesar at Thapsus, after which Numidia became a Roman province. Prince Juba was taken to Rome and paraded in Julius Caesar's Triumphal procession; but he was then raised by Caesar and later by Octavian. Juba learned Latin and Greek and was given a good Greek education: he was said to be erudite and became a prolific writer in Greek. He was also given Roman citizenship. Prince Juba became a friend of Octavian and went with him on military campaigns, becoming an experienced leader. He fought alongside Octavian at Actium.

After his marriage to Cleopatra Selene, Juba was made king of Mauretania (modern Algeria). He and his wife were allowed to take Alexander Helios and Ptolemy Philadelphus with them when they left for their new country, but at that point, the two young princes disappear from the records. In Mauretania, King Juba and Queen Cleopatra Selene founded a new capital city and named it Caesaria (Cherchell, Algeria) in honour of Caesar; and a Royal Mausoleum was built for them at Tipasa (modern Tipaza on the Algerian coast). They both became patrons of the arts and sciences, and under their rule, Mauretania became very prosperous, largely thanks to its access to the *murex* sea snails that were used in their thousands in the production of the costly dye called Tyrian, or imperial, purple. In AD 23, Juba was succeeded by his son, Ptolemy. Seventeen years later, Ptolemy was assassinated on the orders of the Emperor, Caligula - apparently because he had had the temerity to wear in the amphitheatre in Rome a toga that was of a deeper purple that the one worn by the Emperor. Ptolemy had no children and with him the last connection with Cleopatra, the great Queen of Egypt, came to an end.

CHAPTER FIVE

CLEOPATRA IN ART AND DRAMA

Surprisingly, no reliably authenticated contemporary statues of Cleopatra have survived, possibly because after her death they were destroyed. A number of coins were issued during her reign; and on none of them is an image of a beautiful woman shown. This may have been deliberate. Images on coins were stylised and were not intended to be flattering but to convey power, that is, power exerted by men. Cleopatra's coins purposely do not show a beautiful, possibly weak, woman but rather a slightly masculine queen. Her lips and jawline are fleshy and her nose is large and prominent, sometimes represented as sharp and sometimes with a decided hook. In other words, Cleopatra on coins is depicted as a hook-nosed, heavy-jowled Macedonian Greek.

More flattering depictions of Cleopatra are found on the exterior of the rear or southern wall of the main building of the Temple of Hathor at Denderah in Upper Egypt. There are two, one at each end of the wall, mirror images of each other. Each scene depicts Cleopatra with her son by Julius

Caesar, Caesarion, appearing before the goddess Hathor, who is accompanied by her son, Ihy, the musician-god and sistrum-player *par excellence*. Three other deities are in attendance. Caesarion holds out an incense-burner and Cleopatra shakes a pair of sistra, musical instruments sacred to Hathor.

It is not surprising that Cleopatra allowed herself to be depicted worshipping Hathor, who was the goddess of love and beauty, associated by the Greeks with their own goddess of love and beauty, Aphrodite. Sadly, the depiction of Cleopatra at Denderah gives us no idea of her own beauty. The reliefs simply show a standard Ptolemaic queen with no attempt at portraiture.

Cleopatra in Painting

The Cleopatra of our imagination is influenced by the pictorial representations of her that began during the Renaissance, one of the first of them being Michelangelo's small drawing in black chalk on paper dating to 1533-34 and now in the Casa Buonarroti in Florence. It shows a soulful-looking queen with braided hair and a long, serpentine neck. Her head is twisted to her left and a snake is coiled around her naked breast. The face of the woman in the portrait could be that of any woman; only the snake links her to the Egyptian queen who committed suicide by means of a snake, or asp, bite.

Over a hundred years later, Michel Corneille the Elder (1602-1664), one of the leading French artists of his time, was similarly drawn to the story of Cleopatra's death by the bite of an asp. In an oil painting dating to between 1650 and 1660, and now in the Portland Art Museum, he depicts the queen sitting upright on a couch, her servants hovering in the background. She is stretching out her right hand towards a swarthy man holding the basket containing the asp. Cleopatra, looking dignified and composed, is dressed in a pale salmon pink overdress; a large cloth or blanket of bright royal blue covers her knees. The queen captures the attention partly through the vivid blue of the cloth but mostly by the luminescent paleness of her skin.

The eighteenth-century Venetian artist, Giovanni Battista Tiepolo (1696-1770), was inspired by the famous banquet at which Cleopatra dissolved a pearl in wine in order to impress Antony. *The Banquet of Cleopatra*, an oil on canvas painting that he completed in 1744, is now in the National Gallery of Victoria in Melbourne, Australia. It depicts Cleopatra sitting at a banquet table, her hand holding a pearl above a wine goblet. Antony watches from the opposite end of the table and a group of guests and retainers of all shapes, sizes and colours stand around to witness the event. The setting, the facial features, the style of clothes, and even the table, are all contemporary with Tiepolo and owe nothing to ancient Egypt.

Another episode recounted by Plutarch, the death of Mark Antony, is the subject of an oil on canvas painting dated to 1789 and now in the Memorial Art Gallery, Rochester, New York. It is by the French painter, Bernard Duvivier (1762-1837) and shows Antony lying on his death bed with head flung back. On the right of the picture a group of distraught servants stand grieving; on the left a Roman soldier grasping a sword. These figures are painted in muted tones. At the centre of the painting is Cleopatra, with Octavian's emissary, Proculeius, grasping her arm and pulling her away from Antony. Proculeius wears a bright red plume on his helmet; the colour is echoed in the cloth covering Cleopatra's footstool. At the centre of the picture is Cleopatra herself. She is painted in such a way that she seems to be floodlit, so that the onlooker's eye is immediately drawn to her.

Napoleon's Expedition to Egypt in 1798 was made up not only of an army of soldiers but of a small army of artists, scholars and scientists. The fourteen months that Napoleon spent in Egypt began the scientific examination of its antiquities which laid the foundation of modern Egyptology. The work of one of these men, the French Academician Dominique Vivant, Baron Denon (1747-1825), was to have the most far-reaching effects. Denon made hundreds of sketches of the antiquities of ancient Egypt; and in 1802 published them in his *Voyages dans la Basse et la Haute Égypte (Travels in Lower and Upper Egypt)*. Seven years later, the official record began to appear in the first of the eleven volumes, published between 1809 and 1828, that were to make up the *Description de l'Égypt*, which contains nearly a thousand engravings. Through the superb drawings in these works, scholars everywhere gained access to the discoveries made to date in Egypt; and laypeople had a new world opened up to them. Public interest in ancient Egypt became widespread.

The Islamic countries of the Near East, North Africa and Egypt, with their vast deserts and picturesque cities, where the way of life was almost untouched by the modern world, seemed romantic and mysterious, holding out the promise of sensual delights unknown in the West. The fascination with these countries gave rise to a movement known today as Orientalism, which played an important role in the cultural achievements of Western Europe. Writers and poets such as Coleridge, Byron, Hugo, Flaubert, Baudelaire and Goethe, amongst others, found the Orient a rich source of inspiration, as did painters such as Ingres and Delacroix (see below). Their works were products of their imaginations; it was not until the second half of the nineteenth century that comparative ease of travel allowed later Orientalists such as Gérôme to make the journey to Egypt, North Africa and the Near East to see the wonders of the Orient with their own eyes. By the end of the century, photography had arrived and the Orientalists found themselves outmoded.

Not surprisingly, a favourite subject for Orientalists was the queen who was the epitome of exoticism, Cleopatra. The asp makes an appearance in *Cleopatra and the Peasant,* painted in 1838 by Eugène Delacroix (1798-1863), leader of the French Romantic school of art. On the left of the painting a rough-looking, bearded man holds out the asp in a basket covered by a leopard skin. To the right, Cleopatra sits with her right arm leaning on the arm of a chair, resting her chin in her hand and looking obliquely towards the basket. As with earlier painters, Delacroix has depicted the queen with pale skin, drawing the eye of the onlooker towards her.

The painter who had the most far-reaching effect on perceptions of Cleopatra was Jean-Léon Gérôme (1824-1904), a leader of the Academic art movement in nineteenth-century France. Having made frequent visits to countries throughout the Middle East, including Egypt, Gérôme specialized in historical and Orientalist painting. His visit to Egypt in 1857 resulted in an oil painting based on the meeting between Cleopatra and Caesar recounted by Plutarch in his *Life of Caesar*. Some translations of Plutarch state that the queen's servant, Apollodorus, smuggled her into Caesar's presence wrapped in a carpet; others that she was stowed away in the sort of large bag that can still be found today, one made of carpet material and used to carry salt on camelback.

Gérôme made several versions of the scene but the final work, finished in 1866, shows Cleopatra standing before Caesar in what purports to be a palace but is in fact derived from a plate in a volume from the *Description de l'Égypte* that depicts the temple at Deir el-Medina, on the west bank of the Nile at Luxor. Apollodorus is crouching down clearing away a carpet from which Cleopatra has just emerged. She is poised gracefully and sensuously with her left hand lightly touching his shoulder for support; and is bare breasted with a long skirt split to thigh level in two places revealing her legs - more like a woman of the harem than a regal figure. This painting, known variously as *Cleopatra and Caesar* and *Cleopatra Before Caesar,* could have been considered indecent by the general public in an age of prudery but was allowable because it dealt with historic figures removed from contemporary society by being set in an oriental context. *Cleopatra and Caesar* was eventually purchased by Gérôme's father-in-law, Adolphe Goupil (1806-1893) of Goupil & Cie, the leading art dealership of nineteenth-century France. Copies of it, and other works by Gérôme, were mass-produced by Goupil in the form of engravings and photographs, allowing them to reach more people throughout Europe and the United States. Over time, set designers for theatrical and Hollywood productions featuring Cleopatra looked to Gérôme's painting for inspiration. Since 1990, *Cleopatra and Caesar* has been in the hands of a private collector.

Gérôme's contemporary, Lawrence Alma-Tadema, likewise had a great influence on the Western world's perception of Cleopatra. Alma-Tadema (1836-1912), was born in the Netherlands but settled in England in 1870. He eventually became a British citizen and, in 1870, received a knighthood. He was famous for his depictions of the luxury and decadence of the Roman Empire, but by the mid-1860s, he had recognised that public interest in ancient Egypt was profound and decided that paintings with ancient Egyptian themes would be profitable. Alma-Tadema captured one of the most momentous moments in the history of Rome and Egypt in his painting of the meeting between Antony and Cleopatra at Cydnus in 41 BC, first displayed in 1883 and now in a private collection. In this painting, Cleopatra is shown on her barge lounging in a chair, wearing a diaphanous dress and holding in her hands the crook and the flail, symbols of kingship in ancient Egypt. The front of the chair is decorated with a pair of baboons holding wadjet-eyes. Baboons were representations of the Egyptian god of writing and wisdom, Thoth; the wadjet was the divine eye of the god, Horus. On her head, Cleopatra wears a gold circlet with the royal uraeus serpent in the front. She also wears pearl earrings, possibly an allusion to the infamous episode in which Cleopatra dissolved a pearl in a cup of wine. A leopard skin is partly resting on the arm of the chair and partly draped around her shoulders and across her breast. This may have been a reference to the leopard skins that were worn across the shoulders of a *sem*-priest whose chief duty was to officiate at burial ceremonies. In ancient Egypt the eldest son was responsible for the burial of his father and during the burial ceremony he acted as *sem*-priest. The leopard skin worn by Alma Tadema's Cleopatra might be a reference to this and thus an indication that Cleopatra had buried her father and was therefore entitled to claim his property. Cleopatra sits in a booth draped in shimmering, dull-gold curtains. The top of the structure is garlanded with pink roses, suggesting a heady, sweet perfume, a theme taken up in the depiction of servants in the bottom left corner of the painting, each of whom holds an incense-burner of the type seen in reliefs in ancient Egyptian temples. On the side of the barge is a line of inscription, written in hieroglyphs. It reads, from right to left, *nebet* (the female ruler) *tawy* (of the Two Lands, that is, Egypt) and is followed by Cleopatra's name, in not quite accurate hieroglyphs, written inside a cartouche, the elongated oval shape thought to represent a loop of rope, within which royal names were customarily inscribed. Antony, robed in dazzling white, is shown about to alight from a boat. He peers through a gap in the curtains of Cleopatra's barge, a grim look on his face. Cleopatra sits with her eyes averted, seemingly feigning indifference. In his paintings, Alma-Tadema often showed that he had taken pains to acquire an in-depth archaeological knowledge: *The Meeting of Antony and Cleopatra*, 41 BC, with his use of ancient Egyptian objects and motifs, is no exception.

Gustave Moreau's (1826-98) painting, *Cleopatra*, (1887), now in the Louvre, depicts the queen sitting in a chair naked apart from a band of cloth under her breasts, her pubic area draped with a cloth. Gérôme had portrayed her in a revealing dress. For them, Cleopatra's name was on a par with those of the infamous Roman emperors Nero, Caligula and Heliogabalus, bywords for decadence and sexual excess. Alma-Tadema treated Cleopatra with respect: for him she was regal and dignified. His approach earned him praise for originality; but Cleopatra is still to this day synonymous with exotic beauty and oriental excess.

Cleopatra in Drama

Roman poets of the Augustan Age, such as Virgil, Horace and Propertius, sometimes mentioned Cleopatra in their poems, but they were writing in the reign of Caesar Augustus, formerly Octavian, and were biased against her. The father of English poetry, Geoffrey Chaucer (c.1343-1400), wrote *The Legend of Good Women* in praise of nine women famed for their fidelity in love; Cleopatra, whom he described as being 'fair as is the rose in May'[1] is one of them. Other poets have written about her through the ages, but it is in drama that Cleopatra comes to life.

The first known play about Cleopatra was published in 1594, with an amended version appearing in 1623. It was written by Samuel Daniel (c. 1562-1619), an Elizabethan poet, translator, historian and playwright. *The Tragedie of Cleopatra* was based on Plutarch's narrative of her history and took the form of a drama modelled on the plays of the Roman Stoic philosopher, poet and rhetorician, Seneca the Younger, who wrote nine tragedies in the first century AD. Most of these plays were drawn from Greek mythology but differ from Greek drama in the amount of bloodthirsty detail and exaggerated rhetoric that Seneca uses. They were probably not meant to be performed but to be read aloud to a select audience.

Daniel's *Cleopatra* begins after the death of Antony. Octavius tries to persuade the queen to leave the funerary monument in which she has taken refuge, with the intention of taking her captive to Rome to be paraded in his Triumph. After a magnificent feast, Cleopatra sends for a basket of figs in which is secreted the asp whose bite kills her. The play is deficient in action and marked by speeches of inordinate length written in euphuistic language. It seems that it was never performed and was perhaps intended only to be read: a typical closet drama.

The most famous play about the Egyptian queen is, of course, Shakespeare's *Antony and Cleopatra*, first registered for publication in May 1608 in the Stationers' Register although not actually published until 1623 as part of the First Folio, the complete works of Shakespeare assembled and overseen into print by his fellow actors. It had probably been performed for the first time at Christmas 1606, or perhaps at Christmas a year later. Shakespeare's *Antony and Cleopatra* is set in the period after Julius Caesar's assassination when the Roman Empire was ruled by the three men, Octavius Caesar, Lepidus and Mark Antony, who made up the Triumvirate. Antony, captivated by Cleopatra, has chosen to neglect his responsibilities as Triumvir, preferring to spend his time in Alexandria dallying with the queen. The play begins with one of Antony's followers, Philo, complaining to another, Demetrius, that their general's 'dotage' (infatuation) has resulted in his 'captain's heart' becoming 'the bellows and the fan to cool a gipsy's lust'. As Antony and Cleopatra enter, Philo goes on to exhort Demetrius to behold 'the triple pillar of the world transformed into a strumpet's fool'.[2]

When news arrives that Antony's wife, Fulvia, is dead and that Pompey is raising an army to rebel against the Triumvirate, Antony's sense of duty is roused and he feels compelled to return to Rome. In Antony's absence, Octavius Caesar and Lepidus have been worrying about Pompey's increasing strength. Octavius is critical of Antony for neglecting his duties as a statesman and military officer in order to live a decadent life with Cleopatra. He does not, unlike Philo, call the queen a gipsy and a strumpet, but the inference is there. Upon his arrival in Rome, Antony quarrels with Octavius but realises that an alliance between them will be necessary if they are to defeat Pompey. The two rivals agree that to ensure their loyalty to one another Antony will marry Octavius' sister, Octavia. Enobarbus, Antony's closest friend, predicts that, despite the marriage, Antony will surely return to Cleopatra. In Egypt, Cleopatra learns of Antony's marriage and flies into a jealous rage, demanding that the messenger who has brought the news describe Octavia - how old she is, her disposition, how tall she is, not forgetting the colour of her hair.

The Triumvirs meet Pompey and agree to settle their differences without going into battle. Pompey undertakes to keep the peace in exchange for rule over Sicily and Sardinia. That evening, the four men drink to celebrate their truce. Pompey learns that some of his followers have hatched a plan to assassinate the Triumvirs, thereby delivering Rome and the Empire into Pompey's hands, but Pompey dismisses the scheme as unworthy of his honour. Antony and his new wife, Octavia, depart for Athens. Once they are gone, Caesar breaks his truce, wages war against Pompey, and defeats him. After using Lepidus' army to secure victory, he accuses Lepidus of treason, imprisons him, and confiscates his property. News of this angers Antony, as do reports that Caesar has been speaking out against him in public. He sends Octavia back to Rome to negotiate with her brother.

Antony secretly returns to Alexandria and Cleopatra. When Octavius learns that Antony and Cleopatra have crowned themselves and their children as kings and queens, he declares war on Egypt. Antony elects to fight him at sea, and, despite Enobarbus' objections, allows Cleopatra to command a ship. Antony's forces lose the Battle of Actium when Cleopatra's ship flees and Antony follows, leaving the rest of the fleet leaderless. At first, the despairing Antony accuses Cleopatra of being the cause of his shame. He is quick to forgive her, however. When he hears that Octavius has offered to make a secret treaty with Cleopatra, he decides to fight him and scores an unexpected victory. Antony loses a third battle against Octavius when the Egyptian fleet surrenders; even his friend Enobarbus deserts him and goes over to Octavius' side.

A furious Antony accuses Cleopatra of betrayal and in order to protect herself from his anger she seeks refuge in her Monument in Alexandria. She has a message delivered to Antony informing him that she is dead; and Antony, overcome with grief, attempts to kill himself. The dying Antony is carried to the Monument and dies in his lover's arms. Rather than be captured by the victorious Octavius, Cleopatra kills herself. Octavius returns in triumph to Rome but not before decreeing that Cleopatra 'be buried by her Antony' and observing that 'no grave upon the earth shall clip in it a pair so famous'.[3]

Shakespeare depicts Octavius as a priggish pragmatist. His Antony is a portrait of a great military leader rendered, in Roman eyes, an object of ridicule by becoming 'the fool of love'.[4] Plutarch focused on the life and death of Antony, and Shakespeare might have followed suit, choosing to tell the story of *Antony and Cleopatra* from the male point of view. Instead he elected to give Cleopatra nearly as many lines and speeches as Antony. The climax of the play is not the downfall of Antony, the noble Roman, but the death of Cleopatra.

Shakespeare's Cleopatra is a consummate actress. Her temperament is volatile, she veers between seriousness and playfulness. She can be charming and seductive but also manipulative and emasculating - she is the dominant half of the relationship. She has a sense of humour: 'Can Fulvia die?'[5] she asks, playing on the literal meaning of 'to die' and the figurative expression in which to die meant to achieve sexual satisfaction, a hint that Fulvia is frigid. She sometimes acts like a lovesick teenager rather than the mature woman in her late thirties than she actually was; but she is, as her servant, Charmian, puts it, 'A lass unparalleled'.[6] In the theatre, she has to be. As critic Jesse Green pointed out in reviewing an American production, there is the constant danger that the spectator is left wondering 'why Antony abandons his world-dominance responsibilities for a middle-aged lady in nude Spanx, or why she is so desperate to waylay some warbly grandpa with a combover'.

In the century or so after Shakespeare's version of the life of Cleopatra, other playwrights found inspiration in the story. Twelve years later John Fletcher (1579-1625), in collaboration with Philip Massinger (1583-1640), produced *The False One,* first performed c.1620. The play is set in Egypt during the joint kingship of Cleopatra and her brother, Ptolemy, at the time when Pompey, the great general and erstwhile friend of Julius Caesar but now his bitter rival, is seeking refuge in Egypt. The false one of the title is Septimius, the treacherous Roman who murders Pompey. Caesar arrives in Egypt and orders Septimius to be hanged. The rest of the play tells of how the young Cleopatra entangles Caesar in her charms.

Cleopatra, Queen of Egypt, her Tragedy, a seldom performed drama written by Thomas May (1595-1650), first acted in 1626 and published in 1639, begins before the rupture between Octavius Caesar and Antony. In the penultimate act, Cleopatra is torn between Octavius and Antony; and in the fifth, Antony stabs himself. His hearse is brought before Cleopatra and she sets the asp to her breast.

A play more worthy of performance is *All for Love; or, The World Well Lost,* a tragedy in blank verse adapted from *Antony and Cleopatra* by John Dryden (1631-1700), first acted in 1677 and printed in 1678. The action of the play takes place after the battle of Actium and concerns the struggle of Cleopatra to retain the love of Antony in the face of opposition from his wife, Octavian's sister, Octavia, from Octavian's friend, Dolabella and from one of Antony's generals, Ventidius. Octavian is prepared to come to terms with Antony on condition that he puts aside Cleopatra and returns to his wife. Octavia plants in Antony's mind the suspicion that Cleopatra will transfer her affections to the younger man, Dolabella; and a jealous Antony refuses to accede to Octavian's plans. The rest of the play follows the course set by Shakespeare. The original cast featured Charles Hart, Shakespeare's grandnephew, as Antony and Mrs Boutel (see page 162) as Cleopatra.

Caesar in Egypt, a tragedy by Colley Cibber, was first acted at Drury Lane on 9 December, 1724. Barton Booth (1681-1733) played Caesar, Mrs Oldfield (see page 163) Cleopatra and Mrs Porter (Mary Porter) was cast as Caesar's wife, Cornelia, in this play a more important role than that of Cleopatra. The plot of the play is derived from The False One although Cornelia is said to have been based on the character in La Mort de Pompée, a tragedy written by the great French dramatist, Pierre Corneille (1606-84). Many of the speeches in Caesar in Egypt are direct translations from the French although the action of Cibber's play is less refined than that of Corneille's drama: in Cibber's version, for example, the severed head of Pompey is brought on stage. Many of the speeches in *Caesar in Egypt* are direct translations from the French, notably in the fine discourses between Caesar and Cornelia.

It was to be nearly 170 years after the production of *Caesar in Egypt* before a new play was written about Cleopatra. The somewhat surprising author of this drama was the novelist H. Rider Haggard, of *King Solomon's Mines* and *She* fame. The play was based on Haggard's story *Cleopatra: Being an Account of the Fall and Vengeance of Harmachis*, first published in London in 1889 as an adventure novel.

Harmachis, the protagonist, was a priest of the goddess Isis, charged with the task of overthrowing Cleopatra, ruler of an upstart foreign dynasty, ejecting Greeks and Romans from Egypt and restoring Egypt to its former glory. Haggard adapted his novel for the stage: it was performed in Louisville, Kentucky, in September, 1890, under the title *Harmachio*; and in March the following year at the Windsor Theatre, New York, with a new title, *Cleopatra*. H. Rider Haggard is not best known as a dramatist but his Cleopatra is as exotic as the mysterious white queen, Ayesha, or 'She-who-must-be-obeyed' in his novel, *She* - imperious and haughty.

The latest major play featuring Cleopatra is George Bernard Shaw's *Caesar and Cleopatra*, first performed by Mrs Patrick Campbell's company at the Theatre Royal, Newcastle-upon-Tyne, in March, 1899. Shaw wrote the part of Caesar for Sir Johnston Forbes-Robertson (1853-1937), considered by Shaw to be the greatest Hamlet of the Victorian era and one of the finest actors of his time. Shaw particularly valued the excellence of his diction. Thus it is Caesar who is the protagonist in this play, not Cleopatra. The part of Cleopatra was played by the American-born actress, Gertrude Elliott (1874-1950), who married Forbes-Robertson in 1900.

Caesar and Cleopatra is a play in five acts plus a prologue and an 'Alternative to the Prologue'. In the Prologue, the King of the Egyptian gods, Re, addresses the audience directly and tells the story of Pompey's rivalry with Caesar, their battle at Pharsalis, and Pompey's death at the hands of Lucius Septimius. Re claims that Pompey represented the old Rome, Caesar the new. The gods favoured Caesar because he 'lived the life they had given him boldly'. In the 'Alternative to the

Prologue', the captain of Cleopatra's guard is warned that Caesar is about to invade Egypt. Cleopatra has sought refuge in Syria, driven there by her brother, Ptolemy, her rival for the throne. Her officials plan to ask Caesar to proclaim Cleopatra ruler of Egypt, on the assumption that the young woman would be more biddable than her brother, even though he is only ten years old. They try to find her but are informed by her nurse, Ftatateeta, that she has run away. There is no-one named Ftatateeta in other versions of the Cleopatra story, so it is assumed that she is a character created by Shaw. It is said that he based Ftatateeta on Baroness Louise Lehzen, Queen Victoria's German companion and governess who was a great influence on the queen's life until, as with Cleopatra, her influence was superseded by that of a powerful man, in Victoria's case first Lord Melbourne, then Prince Albert, in Cleopatra's, Julius Caesar.

Act 1 opens with Cleopatra sleeping between the paws of the Sphinx at Giza. Caesar wanders in and addresses the Sphinx. Cleopatra wakes up and replies, startling Caesar who assumes that he is either dreaming or has gone mad if he is hearing a stone monument speak. Cleopatra makes herself known to what she perceives to be a nice old man; and tells him about her fear of the Romans, and especially Caesar. The 'nice old man' persuades her to come back to the palace with him, and when he is greeted by the palace guards shouting 'Hail, Caesar', Cleopatra realises who he is and, sobbing with relief, falls into his arms.

Act 2 is set in the royal palace in Alexandria. Here, Caesar meets the young king, Ptolemy, who is accompanied by his aged tutor, Theodotus, his guardian, Pothinus, and the general of his troops, Achillas. Caesar is courteous to them all but insists that Egypt pay a large tribute to Rome. In return, Caesar offers to settle the dispute between the rivals for the throne by letting them reign jointly. This pleases no-one in the Egyptian party, especially Cleopatra, who is fiercely jealous of Caesar's concern for Ptolemy. The Egyptians threaten military action, which does not concern Caesar until he learns that Achillas has at his disposal a number of troops left behind after an earlier Roman incursion into Egypt. The rest of the act is concerned with Caesar's preparations to defend his position. He orders his military aide, Rufio, to take over the palace and to burn the Roman ships that are moored on the western side of the harbour leaving those on the eastern side available for the return to Rome. Then, instead of taking Ptolemy and his followers prisoner, Caesar allows them to leave. Cleopatra chooses to remain with Caesar.

Caesar tries to concentrate on the coming battle but is constantly distracted by Cleopatra's need for his attention. She enthuses about the youth and handsome appearance of Mark Antony, whom she had met when she was twelve years old when he restored her father to the throne. Caesar chooses not to be offended by the contrast between Antony and his middle-aged, balding self, but instead promises Cleopatra that he will send Antony back to Egypt when he returns to Rome. Meanwhile, Rufio discovers that the ships he had been ordered to destroy are already ablaze, torched by Achillas' troops.

Ptolemy's tutor, Theodotus, rushes in to report that the fire has spread from the ships to the great Library of Alexandria. Caesar is not at all sympathetic but tells the distraught Theodotus that it would be better for the Egyptians to live their lives rather than dream them away by reading books; and furthermore, that the burning library will divert the Egyptians away from attacking Roman troops into trying to put out the fire. At the end of the act, Cleopatra helps Caesar to put on his armour and he goes forth to battle.

Act 3 opens with a sentinel looking out from the quay in front of the palace towards the Pharos, the great lighthouse of Alexandria, which has been occupied by Caesar. Cleopatra's nurse, Ftatateeta, accompanied by Cleopatra's loyal follower, Apollodorus, appears on the scene with several porters carrying bales of carpets from which Cleopatra is meant to select a gift for Caesar. Cleopatra herself arrives demanding that she be taken to visit Caesar, only to be informed by the sentinel that she is a prisoner and ordered back into the palace.

Apollodorus procures a small boat and orders a roll of carpet be loaded into it. In Shaw's version of events, the roll of carpet contains Cleopatra. As the boat arrives at the island on which the Pharos stands, it starts to sink and Apollodorus barely has time to drag it and its contents ashore. When Caesar unrolls the carpet he finds a highly distressed Cleopatra. She is even more upset when Caesar barely gives her a thought, so intent is he on the military situation he finds himself in. Matters are made worse when news of the approaching Egyptian army forces Caesar to try to swim to the Roman boats in the eastern harbour. Apollodorus jumps into the water with him but, on Caesar's orders, Cleopatra, a non-swimmer, has to suffer the indignity of being thrown into the water, where, screaming, she clings on to Caesar until a boat arrives to rescue them.

Act 4 opens during the Egyptian siege of the palace, with Cleopatra and Pothinus, Ptolemy's guardian, arguing over who should rule Egypt when Caesar goes back to Rome. After Cleopatra goes away in order to supervise a feast being arranged for Caesar, Pothinus attempts to turn Caesar against Cleopatra by telling him that she is using him to gain the Egyptian throne. Caesar thinks this a very reasonable plan of action and is not offended. Cleopatra, naturally, is offended and orders Fatatateeta to kill Pothinus. During the feast the sound of a thud is heard - Pothinus' body has been thrown from the roof of the palace. The besieging Egyptians are outraged by the murder and begin to storm the building. Cleopatra admits to responsibility for the killing, and Caesar chides her for indulging in petty vengeance rather than exerting the clemency that he would have shown, thereby avoiding stirring up the enemy. When news arrives that reinforcements have arrived to support the Romans, Caesar leaves to speak to his troops. After his departure, Rufio realises that Ftatateeta was Pothinus' murderer and so he kills her by slitting her throat. Cleopatra discovers the bloodied body of her nurse hidden behind a curtain and realises that she is abandoned and friendless.

Act 5 is an epilogue in which Caesar prepares to depart for Rome. His forces have defeated the Egyptian army, sweeping it into the Nile. The young king, Ptolemy, has been drowned when his barge sank. Caesar appoints Rufio governor of Egypt. Cleopatra arrives dressed in mourning for Ftatateeta and accuses Rufio of her murder. This he readily admits to, saying that it was not out of revenge or for punishment, nor even for justice but because, if left alive, she could have been a menace. Caesar approves Rufio's motive, but Cleopatra remains unforgiving until Caesar promises to send Mark Antony to Egypt. An overjoyed Cleopatra says goodbye.

Shaw's Caesar is a world-weary soldier-philosopher, not unlike what one imagines the real man to have been. His Cleopatra is a young girl, even though in real life she was twenty-one when she met Caesar. By ancient Egyptian standards she would have been considered an adult woman since the age of twelve or thirteen. Shaw chose to depict Cleopatra as a demanding and petulant child, endlessly squabbling with her brother, jealously vying with him for Caesar's attention and, from time to time, displaying a vicious streak. It is left to the actress playing the part to find charm in the character.

CHAPTER SIX

PLAYING CLEOPATRA ON STAGE
AND SCREEN

Drama in England has its roots in the mystery and miracle performances that formed part of religious festivals in many European countries during the Middle Ages. Miracle plays were dramas that revolved around the lives of the saints or the Virgin Mary. From the eleventh century onwards they were often enacted as part of church services until, in the thirteenth century, they became separate entities and were often highlights of public festivals. Mystery plays were made up of stories from the Bible and were performed across Europe during the thirteenth to sixteenth centuries. They were acted by members of the local community, both men and women, wearing their own clothes, and were usually staged on a wagon that could be moved around from place to place.

Out of these religious origins grew the morality plays, popular in Europe during the fifteenth and sixteenth centuries. They were dramatic allegories in which a protagonist was confronted by a series of figures representing personifications of qualities such as beauty, avarice and fellowship, and characters such as angels and God, in his quest to forsake a life of evil and instead follow a godly path. The earliest surviving example in English is the *Castle of Perseverance* (c.1420), and the best-known is *Everyman* (c.1510).

Morality plays represent the transition between drama based on religion to secular, professional theatre. An important role in this development was played by the *Commedia dell'Arte*, which began in Italy in the early sixteenth century and quickly spread throughout Europe, creating a lasting influence on Shakespeare among others. The elaborate courtly entertainment known as a masque was also first developed in Italy in the sixteenth century and it too contributed to the development of the theatre. A masque involved music, singing, dancing and acting set in elaborate staging. This, and the costumes worn by the participants, was often designed by a renowned architect. The masque was meant to flatter the king or nobleman in whose house it was performed. Kings, queens, noblemen and their aristocratic friends took part in the productions but speaking and singing parts were performed by professionals.

The performances of mystery and morality plays by the local citizenry were gradually replaced by dramas enacted by companies of professional players, most of whom were attached to the households of leading noblemen who acted as their patrons. In 1572 any actor who was not a member of a recognised company was labelled a vagabond, the dictionary definition of which is 'an idle wandering beggar or thief'. These companies of players performed for the public outside inns, especially those with galleried courtyards. The plays were enacted on a platform set up in the courtyard, with the audience either standing around the dais, or seated at the windows of the galleries. The oldest pub in London is the George, situated on the Borough High Street in Southwark, not far from London Bridge. The partly timber-framed building, which dates from the first half of the sixteenth century, was damaged by fire and rebuilt in 1677, and is the only surviving galleried coaching inn in the capital. The performances of plays in the precincts of inns where there was ready access to ale and beer inevitably led to drunkenness and rowdy behaviour, at which the City of London authorities were not amused.

Despite the hostility of the authorities, purpose-built theatres began to spring up outwith the City, especially in Southwark, on the south bank of the Thames and therefore beyond the City's jurisdiction. Southwark could be reached from the City either by ferry or by walking across London Bridge. It was infamous for its brothels and gambling dens, for bear-baiting and cockfighting. It epitomised for the City Fathers licentiousness and lack of morals, a place that they suspected was a hotbed of sedition. They viewed the actors who plied their trade there in the same light. Fortunately for the actors, Elizabeth l (reigned 1558-1603) and later her successor, James I (reigned 1603-1625), had a fondness for plays, as did members of her Privy Council. In spite of this, the companies had to pretend that their public performances were rehearsals for their frequent appearances before the Queen. She even had her own company, the Queen's Men. The royal performances generated prestige but it was the public performances that generated income.

In 1576 the large refectory of a former Dominican priory in the City of London was adapted for the use of child actors associated with the Queen's chapel choirs who became known as the Children of the Chapel Royal. Dominican monks were known as black friars after the colour of their habits, hence first the monastery and later the theatre was known as Blackfriars. In 1596, the upper floors of the priory were purchased by James Burbage (1531-1597), the leader of a company of players who toured England as the Earl of Leicester's Men, who had realised that rather than lead a peripatetic existence it would be beneficial, both financially and artistically, if the company owned its own playhouse. In later years, Blackfriars playhouse was known simply as The Theatre.

Eleven years earlier, a property on the south bank of the Thames was leased by a local businessman and property developer named Philip Henslowe. John Griggs, a carpenter, built a theatre for him on the site and in 1587 it was opened and named the Rose. The Rose, incidentally, was the first purpose-built playhouse to stage a production of any of Shakespeare's plays. It was used by several acting companies, notably Lord Strange's Men, until, in 1594, Richard Burbage, son of James, formed a new company known as the Lord Chamberlain's Men. Shakespeare seems to have arrived in London about two years earlier, quickly establishing himself as both an actor and a playwright. In 1594 he became a shareholder in the Lord Chamberlain's Men, which was to become one of the most popular acting companies in London, and remained a member of this company for the rest of his career. In 1599, Shakespeare and the Lord Chamberlain's Men opened another playhouse on the outskirts of London, the Globe. When King James came to the throne, Shakespeare and his fellow players were granted a royal licence as the King's Men; and it was as a King's Man that Shakespeare wrote *Antony and Cleopatra,* first performed in the Blackfriars Theatre in 1606.

At this time, women were forbidden to appear on the stage, so female parts had to be acted by boys apprenticed to the actors' companies. Several of Shakespeare's plots required the female lead to disguise herself as a boy, thus boy actors playing Viola in *Twelfth Night,* Rosamund in *As You Like It* and Portia in *The Merchant of Venice* could divest themselves of female attire, in which they may not have been comfortable, and take to the stage for large parts of the play dressed in male costume. Shakespeare tailored his plays to suit the talents of his players; when he wrote *Antony and Cleopatra* he must have had a gifted boy in the company to whom he could entrust the demanding part of Cleopatra.

Shakespeare's Cleopatra is a notoriously difficult part to play: the character goes through a kaleidoscope of emotions, spinning from flirtatiousness to vindictiveness, from joy to anguish, and at the end figuring in a long death-bed scene. For a young boy actor the role must have seemed daunting, although, if he needed a role model for a strong queen, he could look to the late Elizabeth Tudor herself, who, in 1588, famously declared in her speech to her troops at Tilbury before the encounter with the Spanish Armada, that she had the heart and stomach of a king.

Shortly after the English Civil War (1640-46) began, Protestants opposed to the supposed immoralities of the theatre seized their opportunity and in 1642 the Puritan Parliament banned all performances. The ban stayed in place until the Restoration of Charles II (reigned 1660-1685), who was a keen theatre-goer. He awarded royal patents to Sir William Davenant and Sir Thomas Killigrew, giving them the monopoly of public theatre performances. In 1662, Charles took the momentous step of issuing a royal warrant declaring that henceforward all female roles should be performed by actresses. Davenant and Killigrew began casting women almost immediately and their appearance on stage was quickly accepted.

The first professional actress to perform on the English stage is thought to have been Margaret Hughes (*c.*1630-1719), the mistress of Prince Rupert of the Rhine (1619-1682), a cousin of the King and a leading Royalist general in the Civil War. She made her debut on 8th December, 1660, playing Desdemona in Shakespeare's *Othello* for Killigrew's new King's Company. Some ten years later, she left the company for the sake of Prince Rupert, but in 1676 she came out of retirement and spent a year with the Duke's Company, appearing in eight different productions, including *Antony and Cleopatra*, in which she played not Cleopatra but her attendant, Charmian.

Margaret Hughes was the first of many actresses who were the mistresses of powerful men. The most famous of them was Nell Gwynn (1650-1687), who, at the age of thirteen, was employed at the King's Theatre as an orange seller until, a year later, she made her debut on stage. She became the most famous actress of the Restoration period, acknowledged for her comic talent. The native wit of the woman Samuel Pepys called 'pretty, witty Nell' endeared her to Charles II, who is thought to have made her his mistress in 1668, a position she occupied until the King's death in 1685.

In 1791, one of the most famous actresses of the eighteenth century, Dorothea Jordan (1761-1816), became the mistress of William, Duke of Clarence, later King William IV. She lived with him at Bushy House and together they produced at least ten illegitimate children. After their separation in 1811 she was given a yearly stipend on condition that she never again appeared on stage; but in 1814 she broke the agreement and returned to the stage to help pay off the debts of one of her sons-in-law. William cancelled the stipend; and less than two years later she died in poverty in France. Another royal mistress, Lily Langtree (1853-1929), was more fortunate. In 1877, her beauty and charm brought her to the attention of Edward, Prince of Wales. She was a married woman but fortunately for the lovers Lily had a complaisant husband who, thanks to the legendary amounts of money Edward spent on his mistress, chose to turn a blind eye to the affair in favour of enjoying the lavish lifestyle Edward's largesse provided. Lily parted from Edward in 1879, her lover having been captivated by Sarah Bernhardt (1844-1923), the French actress regarded as one of the finest of the nineteenth century. At the suggestion of Oscar Wilde, Lily herself became an actress. In 1890 she played Cleopatra at the Royal Princess's Theatre in Oxford Street, London. Her legendary beauty did not save her from being overwhelmed by the production. In the same year, 'the divine Sarah' played Cleopatra to much better effect thanks to her greater gifts and experience as an actress. Unlike poor Dorothea Jordan, neither Sarah nor Lily died in poverty.

The first actress to play Cleopatra on stage is thought to have been Elizabeth Boutell, (early 1650s?-1715), who, in about 1670, joined the King's Company, then managed by one of the greatest English actors of the age, Thomas Betterton. Eight years later she appeared as Cleopatra in a production of Dryden's *All For Love* (see page 146), which Dryden had adapted from Shakespeare's *Antony and Cleopatra* so that the play better reflected the tastes of the contemporary audience, the focus of the drama being on the conflict between love and honour. Mrs Boutell was said to have been described by Betterton as being a considerable actress, of short stature with agreeable features and a voice that, though weak, was mellow. She had a childish look and was adept at portraying young, innocent ladies. Presumably, Mrs Boutell brought these characteristics into her performance as Cleopatra, stamping her own authority onto the role.

A revival of *All for Love* was staged in 1704, with Elizabeth Barry (1658-1713) playing Cleopatra. Mrs Barry had a gift for playing heroines in Restoration comedies, but her greatest gift was as a tragic actress renowned for her ability to project pathos. In his autobiography Colley Cibber noted that in the art of exciting pity she had a power beyond all the actresses he had yet seen. Cibber was struck by the beauty of her voice which, according to him, could show the most affecting melody and softness that could be imagined - a recommendation for the part of Cleopatra who was also known for the beauty of her voice. Mrs Barry was often described as being plain: her portraits show a heavy-set, heavy-featured woman with a prominent nose. Nevertheless, an anonymous admirer claimed that though she was the ugliest woman in the world off-stage she was the finest woman in the world on it. Undoubtedly her Cleopatra would have been full of passion and pathos.

Some twenty years later, on 9 December, 1724, Anne Oldfield (1683-1730) was to play the part of Cleopatra in Cibber's own drama, *Caesar in Egypt* (see page 147). Mrs Oldfield excelled in both tragic and comic parts; her Cleopatra was said to be her finest role. Tragedies were written specifically for her, such as *The Tragedy of the Lady Jane Grey* by Nicholas Rowe.

In the nineteenth century, *Antony and Cleopatra* was regarded not so much as an opportunity for fine acting but rather as a vehicle for spectacle and pageantry. For over a century the amended versions of Shakespeare's plays written by Nahum Tate, Colley Cibber and David Garrick dominated the stage and it was not until the actor Samuel Phelps (1804-78) took up theatrical management that the fashion changed. In 1844, Phelps took over the Sadler's Wells theatre in Rosebery Avenue, Clerkenwell. The theatre, which had been founded in 1683 by Richard Sadler and named after Sadler and the mineral springs that were found on the property, had been the second new theatre to be opened after the Restoration, the first being the Theatre Royal in Drury Lane. By the mid-18th century, Drury Lane and the other Theatre Royal, at Covent Garden, severely affected the fortunes of other theatres, and it was not until 1843 that the passing of the Theatres Act broke the duopoly.

Between 1844 and 1862, Phelps mounted productions of nearly all of Shakespeare's plays, the most admired of which were *Macbeth* in 1844, *Antony and Cleopatra* in 1849 and *Pericles, Prince of Tyre* in 1854. All were faithful to their original versions. Phelps's best known actress was Isabella Glyn (1823-89), who made notable appearances as Lady Macbeth and Cleopatra. Her Cleopatra was praised for the grace, dignity and classical style of the actress; and for the sublime way in which she played her death scene.

During the Edwardian era, the actor/manager Sir Herbert Beerbohm Tree (1852-1917) made Her Majesty's Theatre, Haymarket, London, famous for its Shakespearean productions. On 27 December, 1906, he mounted an extravagant revival of *Antony and Cleopatra*, with Tree himself playing Antony. His Cleopatra was Constance Collier (1878-1955), a tall, darkly handsome woman noted for her ability to project the force of her personality. As Cleopatra she was robed and crowned in silver and her energetic performance was critically acclaimed. Far from being overwhelmed by the lavish spectacle of the production, she more than held her own. Constance Collier was noted for the purity of her diction and in the 1920s she became a voice coach in Hollywood, helping several actresses to make the transition from silent movies into talking pictures.

One of the greatest actresses to play Cleopatra was Edith Evans. She was born in 1888 and died in 1976, meaning that there are people alive today who remember her, especially for her haughty Lady Bracknell in Oscar Wilde's *The Importance of Being Earnest* and the imperiousness with which she exclaimed 'A handbag!'. In 1925, already a leading actress known for her gift for Restoration comedy, she joined the company of the Old Vic in London to play an impressive range of parts - Portia in *The Merchant of Venice*, Katherina in *The Taming of the Shrew,* Rosalind in *As You Like It*, Mistress Page in *The Merry Wives of Windsor*, and Beatrice in *Much Ado About Nothing*, all feisty females. She also played the Nurse in *Romeo and Juliet* - one of her most celebrated roles - and Cleopatra, although many considered that her true bent was for playing comedy rather than tragedy. Never considered to be good looking, she was able to convey the impression that she was, which satisfied those who expected Cleopatra to be beautiful. In 1946, at the age of fifty-eight, Edith Evans played Cleopatra for the last time, at the Piccadilly Theatre, London, with Godfrey Tearle, well known for being the quintessential English gentleman, as her Antony. Her performance was not universally acclaimed: the influential theatre critic, Kenneth Tynan, thought it was as though Lady Bracknell had been involved in a sordid Alexandrian scandal. In the same year, Edith Evans was made a Dame Commander of the British Empire for services to drama.

One actress who certainly did not have to convey the impression that she was beautiful was Vivien Leigh (1913-1967), although she often felt that her beauty was a handicap that sometimes prevented her from being taken seriously. In 1939, in the face of competition from dozens of actresses, she won the role of Scarlett O'Hara in the film *Gone with the Wind,* for which she won an Academy Award for Best Actress. She won another Academy Award in 1951 for her Blanche Dubois in *A Streetcar Named Desire.*

Despite her great success in these films, in which she went from the vivaciousness of Scarlett to the vulnerability of Blanche, Leigh thought of herself as a stage actress and rather disparaged the cinema, regarding it as a lesser art form. In 1951, she and her husband, Laurence Olivier, appeared together at the St James's Theatre, London, playing the leads in Shakespeare's *Antony and Cleopatra* and Shaw's *Caesar and Cleopatra*, performing each play on alternate nights. Leigh had already made a successful appearance as Cleopatra in the 1946 film *Caesar and Cleopatra* (see page 175) but she was initially reluctant to tackle Shakespeare's Cleopatra on stage, doubtful about her ability to play the part. Olivier persuaded her to do so. In a letter later published in 2004, their fellow actor, John Gielgud, wrote of his fear that 'Viv will never be able to touch the part'; and Harold Nicholson, in his *Diaries and Letters*, published in 1968, recorded that at the time his opinion was that though she was 'beautiful to look at' she was 'not grand enough for so superb a part'. In spite of these reservations, the reviews were mostly positive, with the headline to Ivor Brown's review in the *Observer* proclaiming in the words of Charmian that, like Cleopatra herself, Leigh was 'a lass unparalleled'. The critics were even more flattering when the play transferred to New York, with Brooks Atkinson in the *New York Times* claiming that Leigh was superb. Leigh's Cleopatra developed from the kittenish in the Shaw version to the *femme fatale* in Shakespeare's, in which she was not only beautiful but beguiling, convincingly seducing her Antony with her sex appeal.

Two years after the Oliviers played *Antony and Cleopatra*, Michael Redgrave and Peggy Ashcroft (1907-91) starred in a production at the Royal Shakespeare Theatre in Stratford-upon-Avon. Ashcroft was forty-six years old at the time: twenty-three years earlier she had appeared in a controversial production of *Othello* at the Savoy Theatre, London, playing Desdemona to the Othello of Paul Robeson, the great African-American actor and singer. Ashcroft was appalled to receive hate mail for appearing on stage with a black actor, but that did not prevent her from having a brief affair with him. Among those impressed by Ashcroft's luminous performance as Desdemona was John Gielgud. In 1932, when he was asked by the Oxford University Dramatic Society to direct a production of *Romeo and Juliet*, he invited Ashcroft to play Juliet, with Edith Evans as the nurse. They received rave reviews, and Ashcroft was hailed as the finest Juliet of her generation. She was to become known for her portrayal of all of Shakespeare's young leading women, what she termed his 'golden girls'. For the whole of her career she was characterised by her inner serenity and a seemingly naive and trusting quality. Some thought that she could sometimes be too genteel, an archetypal English middle class lady. For those who remember Ashcroft when she was in her seventies, first playing the saintly English lady in David Lean's film of E. M. Forster's novel *A Passage to India*, and then playing the self-doubting former missionary in the television production of *The Jewel in the Crown*, based on Paul Scott's *Raj Quartet*, this would seem to be the case. But Ashcroft's Cleopatra was red-haired and displayed the fiery temperament supposedly typical of those with that hair colour. She went from being childlike to a furiously jealous woman, and ended as a great and noble queen. Three years after her appearance as

of appreciative whistles.' Shulman went on to say that in her 'taunting, kittenish treatment of Antony, Mirren pouted and sighed to good effec' but noted that she displayed little of 'the regal eroticism that made Cleopatra a symbol of feminine mystery and power. Her death scene, too, seemed a very small affair.'

At twenty years old, Mirren was undoubtedly too young to play Cleopatra. Time, however, took care of that; and she remained an actress who was unselfconsciously sensual, well aware of the effect she had on men. In 1982, a thirty-seven-year-old Mirren played Cleopatra again, this time at the Royal Shakespeare Company's studio theatre in Stratford-upon-Avon. Her Cleopatra was intelligent, volatile, erotic, sometimes funny and finally majestic and tragic in death. Mirren gave a magnificent display of Cleopatra's 'infinite variety'. In the 1998 production of *Antony and Cleopatra* at the National Theatre in London, she was less successful, garnering some of the worst reviews of her career. It might have been expected that Mirren and her Antony, Alan Rickman, would have struck sparks off each other: Rickman was, after all, noted for his portrayal of screen villains in films such as *Die Hard*, the Harry Potter series and *Robin Hood, Prince of Thieves*, in which his manic Sheriff of Nottingham steals every scene. Expectations were confounded. Nicholas de Jongh, in his review in the *Evening Standard*, complained that 'they rose to erotic ardour… with little more enthusiasm than a pair of glumly non-mating pandas at London Zoo, coaxed to do their duty to perpetuate the species.'

Janet Suzman (born 1939), made a DBE in 2011, appeared as Cleopatra for the Royal Shakespeare Company in 1972, in an intelligent, athletic performance that was considered by many to be definitive. She is known for playing strong, imperious women, qualities that she brought to her Cleopatra. Suzman is also known for her strong political opinions so it was no surprise that her Cleopatra was politically astute. Another actress with political opinions is Glenda Jackson (born 1936), who gave up the stage to become a Member of Parliament in 1992. She resigned her seat in 2015 and a year later, at the age of eighty, played King Lear in what was thought to be an astonishing interpretation of one of the most demanding parts that Shakespeare ever wrote. Her Cleopatra, which she played at the Royal Shakespeare Theatre in 1978, was noted for her tough, forthright presentation of a politically aware and decidedly unromantic queen, whose Antony, Alan Howard, was judged by some to be more physically attractive than she was. Seven years previously, the unstuffy Jackson had played Cleopatra on the Morecambe and Wise Show in a version of *Antony and Cleopatra* 'what Ernie Wise wrote'.

Judi Dench (born 1934, made a DBE in 1988) is thought by many to be the greatest stage actor of modern times. Her finest performances range from her twinkly-eyed Beatrice in the 1976 production of *Much Ado about Nothing* at the Royal Shakespeare Theatre to her haunted appearance as Lady Macbeth in the same season. In 1987, Peter Hall asked her to play Cleopatra in a production at the National Theatre. Her initial response to his invitation is said to have been, 'I hope you know what you are doing. You are setting out to direct Cleopatra with a menopausal dwarf.' The diminutive fifty-three-year-old Dench wasn't going to grow any taller: but she imbued her Cleopatra with all her own qualities and personality. She turned from languor to humour to melancholy to vanity, all in an instant. Nearly twenty years later, Dench was to become famous for playing M, James Bond's boss, in *GoldenEye*, released in 1995. She played M in another six Bond films, ending in 2012 with *Skyfall*. In 1998, she appeared as Queen Elizabeth I in *Shakespeare in Love*: it was only a cameo performance but it was enough to win her an Oscar for Best Supporting Actress.

Another National Treasure, Maggie Smith, best known today as the formidable Dowager Countess of Grantham in the ITV series *Downton Abbey*, and earlier for her idealistic teacher in the 1969 film, *The Prime of Miss Jean Brodie*, is less known for her witty portrayal of Cleopatra in 1976 at the Stratford Festival in Canada. Yet another National Treasure, this time male, is Captain Jean-Luc Picard, otherwise known as Patrick Stewart, Antony in the Royal Shakespeare Theatre's 2006 production of *Antony and Cleopatra*. His leading lady was Harriet Walter (born 1950, made DBE in 2011). Stewart's Antony was a grizzled old soldier, only truly at ease in the company of his army comrades. Walter's Cleopatra was supple and dynamic, clearly more intelligent than Antony, who was quickly enmeshed in her coils.

There have been many other actresses who have played Cleopatra over the years, the most unexpected of whom may be Kim Cattrall, who starred in the American television series, *Sex and the City*, between 1998 and 2004. Cattrall, often called 'a sultry actress', was born in Liverpool in 1956. She returned to the city in 2010 to star in the Liverpool Playhouse production of *Antony and Cleopatra*, after which her father is said to have called her 'the Liverpool Cleopatra', although there is no suggestion that she played the part in a Scouse accent. Another star of an American television series is the English actress, Eve Best (born 1971), who played the free-spirited Doctor O'Hara in *Nurse Jackie*, which ran from 2009 to 2015. In 2014, Best played Cleopatra at the Globe Theatre. She was mercurial and inventive: she came down from the stage each night to kiss a man in the audience, although it is doubtful that the real Cleopatra would have deigned to do so.

In 2017, the Royal Shakespeare Theatre staged the latest in its long line of productions of *Antony and Cleopatra*, with Josette Simon playing Cleopatra. Simon, who is of Antiguan descent, made her debut with the Royal Shakespeare Company in 1982, when she was in her early twenties. At that time no black actress had played a Shakespearean heroine with the Company. Simon was soon to play Rosalind in *As You Like It*, Titania in *Midsummer Night's Dream* and Isabella in *Measure for Measure,* demonstrating the range of her abilities. In her first season, Simon played handmaiden to Helen Mirren's Cleopatra. Like Mirren, she had been offered the part in her early twenties. Unlike Mirren, she turned it down, feeling that it was not the right time for her to play Cleopatra. Three decades later, Michael Billington, the *Guardian*'s theatre critic, was inspired to say in his review on 24 March, 2017 that 'Simon seems born to play Cleopatra.' Her Cleopatra prowled around the stage restlessly, her long, lithe limbs demonstrating a feline grace. Simon's performance was to some eyes physical to the detriment of the poetry in the lines she spoke. Her co-star, Antony Byrne, was especially good at portraying Antony as the self-proclaimed 'plain, blunt man'. The proposed 2018 production of the play at the National Theatre promises interesting aspects of the heroine, who is to be played by another black actress, Sophie Okonedo. She made a notable appearance in the 2012 television production of *The Hollow Crown*, an adaptation of Shakespeare's history plays, as Margaret of Anjou, fearsome wife of Henry VI. Okenado's Antony is to be Ralph Fiennes, best known to many as the terrifying Lord Voldemort in the Harry Potter films. Queen Margaret seducing Lord Voldemort may prove interesting.

CLEOPATRA IN THE CINEMA

The first screen version of Cleopatra's story was the 1910 black and white silent film, *Cleopatre*, made in France and starring Madeleine Roch, one of the stars of the Comédie-Francaise Theatre in Paris from 1903 until her death in 1930. She evidently brought her gift for playing tragedy to the part, but, of course, the narrative was pictorial. Seven years later, another black and white silent film was made, for the Fox Film Corporation in America. It was given the title *Cleopatra* and the story-line was based on H. Rider Haggard's 1889 novel, *Cleopatra* (see page 147), the 1890 play, *Cleopatre*, written by the French playwrights, Emile Moreau and Victorien Sardou, and Shakespeare's *Antony and Cleopatra*. Its star was Theda Bara (1885-1955), one of cinema's earliest sex symbols and most popular actresses of the silent era, known for her playing of *femme fatale* roles. At the time, the film was one of the most elaborate Hollywood productions ever made, with particularly lavish costumes and sets. Theda Bara appeared in a series of costumes, some of them thought to be bordering on indecent. *Cleopatra* fell victim to the various state and city censorship boards, with cuts demanded of any scenes showing too much flesh, especially breasts, navel or even legs. After the implementation of the Hays Code in 1930, this set of moral guidelines that was laid out for the film industry dictated that *Cleopatra* was too obscene to be shown in public. Sadly, we cannot judge this for ourselves, for only a few fragments remain of the last two surviving prints of the film, which were destroyed in a disastrous fire at the Fox studios in 1937.

Cecil B. DeMille seems to have got round the strictures of the Hays Code in his 1932 historical epic, *The Sign of the Cross*, in which the heroine, played by Claudette Colbert (1903-96) in *femme fatale* mode, bathes nude in a marble pool filled with asses' milk. Not surprisingly, the film was one of Colbert's biggest box-office hits. She was an American actress of French descent who began her career on Broadway in the 1920s and was a leading lady in Hollywood for over two decades. She was known for her low-pitched, musical voice, and in 1928 was signed by Paramount Pictures, which was looking for stage actors who could deliver spoken dialogue in the new talking pictures. Not classically beautiful, she had an apple-cheeked face and high-arched, thinly-plucked eyebrows that set off big eyes; and an elegant, aristocratic manner that conveyed great charm. Over her Hollywood career she displayed a flair not only for emotional drama but also for light, sophisticated comedy.

In 1934, Colbert starred in Cecil B. DeMille's black-and-white epic, *Cleopatra*. The film is noted for its lavish sets and opulent, not quite ancient Egyptian, costumes; and for the scene of Cleopatra's seduction of Antony, which takes place on her barge and has become legendary, with voluptuous sirens being hauled aboard in a giant net so that they might offer Antony oyster-shells filled with jewels. There are dozens of muscular, leopard-skin-clad male dancers, and lithe women cartwheeling through burning hoops. The film is a paean to decadence, an erotic *tour-de-force*. As Cleopatra, Colbert looks beautiful, as might be expected; she also looks exotic, although many of her tight-fitting costumes, some with fishtail hemlines as often worn by Ginger Rogers when she was dancing with Fred Astaire, would not have looked out of place at a 1930s society ball. The dialogue is contemporary, in some scenes redolent of the wisecracking banter heard at the smart cocktail parties that featured in many films of the period. In spite of the lavishness of the production, Colbert is not overwhelmed, giving her Cleopatra intelligence and backbone. As with many of her film roles, Colbert plays a feisty female whose worth is twice that of any man, even a Roman man. In real life, however, Colbert had a failing: she was afraid of snakes, which proved problematic when she had to clutch the asp to her breast for the shooting of her death scene. The death scene is impressive, a fitting end to the film; and to Colbert's career as an exotic *femme fatale* - henceforward she refused to play overtly sexual parts.

In 1946, Shaw's *Caesar and Cleopatra* was brought to the cinema screen: it had been filmed in Technicolour and was at the time the most expensive film ever produced in Britain. It was directed by the Hungarian Gabriel Pascal, famous for filming Shaw's best plays; and the cinematography was by the incomparable Jack Cardiff and Freddie Young. The star of the film was Claude Rains as the world-weary Caesar; but every scene in which he appeared was stolen by the Cleopatra of Vivien Leigh, who fully realised Shaw's perception of the character. On first meeting Caesar, she is a timid, sometimes kittenish, young girl. She develops into a determined, headstrong, intelligent woman who convincingly captures the fancy of the cultivated older man, Caesar. Leigh brought the gifts she displayed in *Gone With the Wind* and translated them into the legendary Queen of Egypt.

What inevitably became the most famous film about Cleopatra was made in 1963. It starred Elizabeth Taylor (1932-2011) as Cleopatra, Richard Burton as Antony and Rex Harrison as Julius Caesar. Harrison, an accomplished actor who was to win an Academy Award in 1964 for his Professor Henry Higgins in *My Fair Lady,* which he had also played on stage, stole the first part of the film. Burton, a very fine Shakespearean actor, was a magnetic Antony. Taylor was considered to be one of the most beautiful women in the world: those who expected the same of Cleopatra were not disappointed. Taylor the famous film star inevitably brought an unrivalled amount of glamour to her Cleopatra; and her personal life informed the film. Her health was frail and she brought a fragile quality to Cleopatra. Her interpretation of the role, however, was overshadowed by the notoriety that surrounded the making of the film. It was rumoured that she, a married woman, was having an affair with her co-star, Burton. The film was also plagued by production troubles, amongst which were problems with the elaborate sets, the lack of a shooting script, a change in director and massive cost overruns. It was the most expensive film that had ever been made and almost bankrupted Twentieth Century Fox. It is recorded, probably apocryphally, that one of the many extras was moved to inquire: 'Who do you sleep with to get out of this movie?'

In 1972, the English actress, Hildegard Neil (born 1939), played Cleopatra in a film written and directed by Charlton Heston, who, of course, played Antony. It contained an unusual number of outdoor scenes, including an epic Battle of Actium, and a chariot race with footage taken from Heston's own *Ben Hur*. Neil did her best with a thankless task; but it must have been daunting to play opposite the embodiment of Moses, Ben Hur and the Cid. The biggest compliment to her performance was an observation that she was a perfect advertisement for Max Factor makeup.

Cleopatra has not always been taken seriously: it was perhaps inevitable that she should feature in one of the British comedy films in the *Carry On* series, and in *Carry On Cleo*, made in 1964, she was brought to life by the blond and buxom Amanda Barrie (born 1935). Asterix the Gaul, the diminutive hero created by Rene Goscinny and Albert Uderzo, who gained superhuman strength after he drank the magic potion made by the druid, Getafix, and who always had a cunning plan, put his talents at the service of the Egyptian queen in *Asterix and Cleopatra*, which was made into an animated film and released in 1968. The original comic book had been released in serial form in the same year as the Hollywood epic and had gently parodied that film's pretensions: the cover claimed the contents to be 'the greatest story ever drawn'. Asterix met up with Cleopatra again in *Asterix & Obelix: Mission Cleopatra*, which was made into a feature film in 2002.

CLEOPATRA ON TELEVISION

Trevor Nunn's production of *Antony and Cleopatra* for the Royal Shakespeare Theatre was adapted for television by Jon Scofield and broadcast on ITV in 1974. Janet Suzman featured as Cleopatra (see page 169). In 1981, *Antony and Cleopatra* was screened as part of the BBC's undertaking to film all of Shakespeare's plays for television. Cleopatra was played by Jane Lapotaire (born 1944) in a gripping performance in which she showed that Cleopatra was not so much physically attracted to Antony as drawn to him for his prowess as a soldier.

Shaw's *Caesar and Cleopatra* was also filmed for television. In a version made in 1976 the Canadian actress, Genevieve Bujold (born 1942), played Cleopatra. Bujold is perhaps best known for her role as Anne Boleyn, second wife and queen to Henry VIII, in the 1969 film *Anne of the Thousand Days*, for which she won the Academy Award for Best Actress. Her young Cleopatra was flirtatious and impulsive, and some preferred her version to that of Vivien Leigh.

Cleopatra is one of the most challenging roles in any medium. Shakespeare's version is especially so: both the language of the play and the complexities of the character have to be coped with. Each actress may be capable of portraying certain aspects but it is rare than any one actress can successfully play all of them. The long final scene is perhaps the greatest test in English drama of an actress's ability. The difficulties of the part are the reasons that great actresses such as Sarah Siddons (1755-1831) and Ellen Terry (1847-1928) seemed to have taken care to avoid the role. Over the centuries, many actresses have accepted the challenge. Some of them, from Boutell to Simon, have appeared in the preceding pages. They each have a different face, a different size and shape, a different voice, some fitting our perceptions of Cleopatra, others, but not all, confirming the statement that Cleopatra was 'a lady of infinite variety'. The role of Cleopatra changed from one that was played by boys to one that was played by actresses who were regarded as women of ill repute. Since the early twentieth century, one of her gifts to the British stage has been the part she has played in helping some actresses to achieve the status of Dame of the British Empire.

CHAPTER SEVEN

CLEOMANIA

The enthusiasm for all things ancient Egyptian goes back a long way. Around 450 BC, Herodotus of Halicarnassus (modern Bodrum in Turkey), the earliest recognized historian and therefore known as the Father of History, spent about two years in Egypt and wrote about all the fascinating things he saw there in Book Two of his great work, *The Histories*. He claimed that Egypt had more amazing monuments than any other country in the world. It had mummies, it had crocodiles, it even had cats that were treated with such reverence that a Greek would open his eyes wide with astonishment. Above all, the Egyptians did everything the wrong way round - they wrote from right to left, unlike the Greeks who did it the proper way. They kneaded dough with their feet and clay with their hands, the women went to market to trade while the men stayed at home and did the weaving, the women urinated standing up, the men sitting down; and both sexes stayed indoors to do so. They ate outside the house, and so on and so on, not always with complete accuracy. Herodotus' readers found the country as fascinating as he did.

The Greek and Roman rulers of Egypt allowed themselves to be portrayed on temple walls dressed in Egyptian fashion and with their names written inside cartouches, but this was largely done as a political statement rather than a demonstration of admiration for Egypt. The Emperor Hadrian (ruled AD117-138) had a large section of his villa in Tivoli, just outside Rome, decorated in the Egyptian style, partly out of admiration for Egypt but also partly to commemorate his young lover, Antinous, who had drowned in the Nile. The Egyptian section of the villa contained Egyptianized statues of Antinous. Some Roman residents of Egypt had themselves mummified in the Egyptian fashion; and many of them worshipped Isis. The worship of Isis spread to the furthest limits of the Roman Empire. In the first century BC, she was perhaps the most popular goddess in Rome. Her cult was superseded only by that of the Virgin Mary; and even then she was not obliterated, for the iconography of Isis, in which she was often depicted with her infant son Horus sitting on her knee, gave rise to depictions of Mary with the infant Jesus on her lap.

With the rise of Islam in the seventh century AD, Egypt was not readily accessible to Europeans. Some of those wishing to journey to Jerusalem, either as pilgrims or as crusaders, made their way there via northern Egypt; otherwise the country remained a mystery. Much of what was known about ancient Egypt was derived from the many objects that the Romans had brought back over a thousand years earlier. Some of them were gathered together by Athanasius Kircher (1602-1680), a German Jesuit scholar and polymath, and displayed in a museum in Rome. Kircher also helped to promulgate interest in ancient Egypt by publishing books containing illustrations of these antiquities. It was not until the eighteenth century that explorers ventured into Egypt to see for themselves what the country contained, although most of them confined their attentions to sites around Cairo. Two who ventured further south were Frederik Norden (1708-1742) and Richard Pococke (1704-1765), who, in 1737, travelled to Egypt independently of one another. Norden was a Danish naval captain who, at the request of King Christian of Denmark, sailed up the Nile as far as the Sudan, making abundant notes, observations, drawings and maps of everything around him, from pharaonic monuments to contemporary architecture, published in the posthumous *Voyage d'Égypte et de Nubie*. Pococke was an Anglican clergyman. His stay in Egypt lasted just over two months, but in that time he managed to draw an amazing number of ancient Egyptian monuments, which, when published, played a major part in stimulating interest in ancient Egypt.

It was Napoleon Bonaparte who instigated the greatest bout of Egyptomania. In 1798, he sailed to Egypt with the intention of conquering it so that he could use it as a base from which to launch an attack on England's prize possession, India. He took with him a number of artists, scientists and scholars and instituted a programme of mapping, exploration, observation and recording, something that had never before been done. He intended that through publication of their findings, Egypt, ancient and modern, would be opened up to the general public. The scientific study of ancient Egypt had begun; and fascination with the subject seems never-ending. Furniture, jewellery and ceramics were produced, made 'in the Egyptian style'; buildings began to exhibit ancient Egyptian architectural designs. Mass produced clocks, tea sets, hatpins, all in the Egyptian style, became popular. Even cosmetics and soap were made according to what was claimed to be Egyptian recipes. The Wedgewood pottery produced a variety of objects, from trinket boxes to teapots. Their Egyptianware included an especially popular teapot with a crocodile handle on the lid, and the pot itself decorated with cobras, lotus flowers and sphinxes. A similar phenomenon occurred with the discovery of Tutankamun's tomb in 1922, which led to Tutmania.

Cleomania was especially notable in beauty products; after all, Cleopatra had become a universal symbol of feminine beauty. In 1820, Caleb Johnson of the American B. J. Johnson Soap Company invented Palmolive soap, which was a mixture of palm and olive oils, ingredients that the Palmolive advertisements claimed had been used by the women of ancient Egypt. Advertisements in magazines such as the *Ladies' Home Journal* were aimed at convincing readers that thanks to Johnson's Soap Company they could have access to what once had been 'a queen's secret' and enjoy the 're-incarnation of beauty'. Other soaps have been produced named after the queen.

One of the most popular cigarettes in Egypt is called 'Cleopatra'. Caesar's Palace nightclub in Las Vegas has within it a floating bar called 'Cleopatra's Barge'. There is an online casino game called Cleo; and there is an asteroid called Cleopatra: its two moons are named after her twins,

Alexander Helios and Cleopatra Selene. Songs have been composed about her: one somewhat outlandish one, entitled *Cleopatra Had a Jazz Band* was composed in 1917 by Jack Coogan and Jimmy Morgan. Its lyrics contain the immortal lines:

> Cleopatra had a jazz band
> In her castle on the Nile,
> Ev'ry night she gave a jazz dance
> In her queer Egyptian style;
> She won Mark Anthony
> With her syncopated harmony ...
> But the real Historic scandal was,
> Cleopatra lost her sandal,
> As she danced to the strains of the Egyptian Jazz Band tune.

After the pyramid the most well-known symbol of ancient Egypt is the obelisk, the tall, tapering pillar of granite, cut from the bedrock as a single piece of stone, that was erected before the entrance to a temple. The modern word for the structure, in English and in most languages, is derived from the Greek *obeliskos*, meaning 'little spit' (skewer for roasting meat). The Arabic word, *messalah*, is perhaps a more accurate term - it means 'darning needle'. King Thutmose III (1479-1426 BC) commissioned two obelisks for erection before the Temple of the Sun at Heliopolis (near modern-day Cairo) to commemorate the Jubilee he celebrated in the thirty-seventh year of his reign (about 1442 BC). Some two hundred years later, Ramesses II (1279-1213 BC) had inscriptions of his own added to the obelisks. The obelisks remained at Heliopolis for some fifteen centuries before the Emperor Augustus (Octavian) ordered them to be removed to Alexandria and erected at the Caesarium, the temple of the deified Julius Caesar. There they remained until one of them fell in an earthquake in AD 1301. Napoleon intended to have both obelisks taken to France, but his plan was thwarted when he was forced out of Egypt after Nelson's victory at the Battle of the Nile in 1798. The standing obelisk was eventually taken to New York, where it was erected in Central Park. Paris boasts its own obelisk, one of a pair from the Temple of Luxor dating to the reign of Ramesses II, which stands in the Place de la Concorde. In 1820, the ruler of Egypt, Mohammed Ali, offered the fallen obelisk from Alexandria to King George IV on his accession to the British throne. The gift remained unclaimed until Prince Albert pressed for the obelisk to be brought to London. It arrived in England in January, 1878, and was erected on the Thames Embankment in the City of Westminster. The red granite obelisk stands about 21 metres (69 ft) high, and weighs about 224 tons. Beneath it is a time capsule containing, amongst other things, photographs of twelve pretty Englishwomen.

Each of the three obelisks, inevitably, is called 'Cleopatra's Needle', even though Cleopatra was born centuries after they were carved out of the granite quarries at Aswan. It seems apt, however, that one icon of ancient Egypt, the obelisk, should be instrumental in gaining immortality for another, Cleopatra, and not just because it has been named in her honour. The ancient Egyptians believed in an Afterlife, and thought that the preservation of the body was necessary to enable a dead person to live in it. If the body were destroyed, a statue or relief of the dead person could stand in for it. If all else failed, then pronouncing a dead person's name would suffice to ensure his or her continuing existence in the Afterlife. It is somehow comforting to think that every time a tourist visits one of 'Cleopatra's needles' and utters the name, Cleopatra, according to ancient Egyptian belief, is being ensured of immortality.

Appendices 1 and 2 in the following pages have been added to the book to allow readers to read for themselves the tone and style, and sometimes the invective, in which Cicero and Dio Cassius wrote about Antony. Appendix 3 gives the reader ready access to Dio Cassius' account of the brilliant, often funny, defence of Antony by his friend Calenus. Similarly, Appendix 4 allows the reader access to Josephus' account of the behaviour of Antony and Cleopatra, whilst Appendix 5 is the complete version of Plutarch's description of the death of Cleopatra and Octavian's reaction to it which formed the basis of the version related in the book. Appendix 6 is a brief resume of the gods and goddesses of the period who are referred to in the book. Good translations of the classical authors can be found online under Project Gutenberg.

APPENDIX I

Cicero's Letter Number 34 to M. Junius Brutus in Macedonia
ROME (MIDDLE OF JULY)

You have Messalla with you. What letter, therefore, can I write with such minute care as to enable me to explain to you what is being done and what is occurring in public affairs, more thoroughly than he will describe them to you, who has at once the most intimate knowledge of everything, and the talent for unfolding and conveying it to you in the best possible manner? For beware of thinking, Brutus - for though it is unnecessary for me to write to you what you know already, yet I cannot pass over in silence such eminence in every kind of greatness - beware of thinking, I say, that he has any parallel in honesty and firmness, care and zeal for the Republic. So much so that in him eloquence - in which he is extraordinarily eminent - scarcely seems to offer any opportunity for praise. Yet in this accomplishment itself his wisdom is made more evident; with such excellent judgment and with so much acuteness has he practised himself in the most genuine style of rhetoric. Such also is his industry, and so great the amount of midnight labour that he bestows on this study, that the chief thanks would not seem to be due to natural genius, great as it is in his case. But my affection carries me away: for it is not the purpose of this letter to praise Mesalla, especially to Brutus, to whom his excellence is not less known than it is to me, and these particular accomplishments of his which I am praising even better. Grieved as I was to let him go from my side, my one consolation was that in going to you who are to me a second self, he was performing a duty and following the path of the truest glory. But enough of this. I now come, after a long interval of time, to a certain letter of yours, in which, while paying me many compliments, you find one fault with me - that I was excessive and, as it were, extravagant in proposing votes of honour. That is your criticism: another's, perhaps, might be that I was too stern in inflicting punishment and exacting penalties, unless by chance you blame me for both. If that is so, I desire that my principle in both these things should be very clearly known to you. And I do not rely solely on the dictum of Solon, who was at once the wisest of the Seven and the only lawgiver among them. He said that a state was kept together by two things - reward and punishment. Of course there is a certain moderation to be observed in both, as in everything else, and what we may call a golden mean in both these things. But I have no intention to dilate on such an important subject in this place.

But what has been my aim during this war in the motions I have made in the senate I think it will not be out of place to explain. After the death of Caesar and your ever memorable Ides of March, Brutus, you have not forgotten what I said had been omitted by you and your colleagues, and what a heavy cloud I declared to be hanging over the Republic. A great pest had been removed by your means, a great blot on the Roman people wiped out, immense glory in truth acquired by yourselves: but an engine for exercising kingly power had been put into the hands of Lepidus and Antony, of whom the former was the more fickle of the two, the latter the more corrupt, but both of whom dreaded peace and were enemies to quiet. Against these men, inflamed with the ambition of revolutionising the state, we had no protecting force to oppose. For the fact of the matter was this: the state had become roused as one man to maintain its liberty; I at the time was even excessively warlike; you, perhaps with more wisdom, quitted the city which you had liberated, and when Italy offered you her services declined them. Accordingly, when I saw the city in the possession of parricides, and that neither you nor Cassius could remain in it with safety, and that it was held down by Antony's armed guards, I thought that I too ought to leave it: for a city held down by traitors, with all opportunity of giving aid cut off, was a shocking spectacle. But the same spirit as always had animated me, staunch to the love of country, did not admit the thought of a departure from its dangers. Accordingly, in the very midst of my voyage to Achaia, when in the period of the Etesian gales a south wind - as though remonstrating against my design - had brought me back to Italy, I saw you at Velia and was much distressed: for you were on the point of leaving the country, Brutus - leaving it, I say, for our friends the Stoics deny that wise men ever 'flee'. As soon as I reached Rome I at once threw myself in opposition to Antony's treason and insane policy: and having roused his wrath against me, I began entering upon a policy truly Brutus-like - for this is the distinctive mark of your family - that of freeing my country. The rest of the story is too long to tell, and must be passed over by me, for it is about myself. I will only say this much: that this young Caesar, thanks to whom we still exist, if we would confess the truth, was a stream from the fountain-head of my policy. To him I voted honours, none indeed, Brutus, that were not his due. none that were not inevitable. For directly we began the recovery of liberty, when the divine excellence of even Decimus Brutus had not yet bestirred itself sufficiently to give us an indication of the truth, and when our sole protection depended on the boy who had shaken Antony from our shoulders, what honour was there that he did not deserve to have decreed to him? However, all I then proposed for him was a complimentary vote of thanks, and that too expressed with moderation. I also proposed a decree conferring imperium on him, which, although it seemed too great a compliment for one of his age, was yet necessary for one commanding an army - for what is an army without a commander with imperium? Philippus proposed a statue; Servius at first proposed a license to stand for office before the regular time. Servilius afterwards proposed that the time should be still farther curtailed. At that time nothing was thought too good for him.

But somehow men are more easily found who are liberal at a time of alarm, than grateful when victory has been won. For when that most joyful day of Decimus Brutus' relief from blockade had dawned on the Republic and happened also to be his birthday, I proposed that the name of Brutus should be entered in the fasti under that date. And in that I followed the example of our ancestors, who paid this honour to the woman Laurentia, at whose altar in the Velabrum you pontiffs are accustomed to offer service. And when I proposed this honour to Brutus I wished that there should be in the fasti (the Calendar of events) an eternal memorial of a most welcome victory: and yet on that very day I discovered that the ill-disposed in the senate were somewhat in a majority over the grateful. In the course of those same days I lavished honours - if you like that word - upon the dead Hirtius, Pansa, and even Aquila. And who has any fault to find with that, unless he be one who, no sooner an alarm is over, forgets the past danger? There was added to this grateful memorial of a benefit received some consideration of what would be for the good of posterity also; for I wished that there should exist some perpetual record of the popular execration of our most ruthless enemies. I suspect that the next step does not meet with your approbation. It was disapproved by your friends, who are indeed most excellent citizens, but inexperienced in public business. I mean my proposing an ovation for Caesar. For myself, however - though I am perhaps wrong, and I am not a man who believes his own way necessarily right - I think that in the course of this war I never took a more prudent step. The reason for this I must not reveal, lest I should seem to have a sense of favours to come rather than to be grateful for those received. I have said too much already: let us look at other points. I proposed honours to Decimus Brutus, and also to Lucius Plancus. Those indeed are noble spirits whose spur to action is glory: but the senate also is wise to avail itself of any means - provided that they are honourable - by which it thinks that a particular man can be induced to support the Republic. But - you say - I am blamed in regard to Lepidus: for, having placed his statue on the rostra, I also voted for its removal. I tried by paying him a compliment to recall him from his insane policy. The infatuation of that most unstable of men rendered my prudence futile. Yet all the same more good was done by demolishing the statue of Lepidus, than harm by putting it up.

Enough about honours; now I must say a few words about penalties. For I have gathered from frequent expressions in your letters that in regard to those whom you have conquered in war, you desire that your clemency should be praised. I hold, indeed, that you do and say nothing but what becomes a philosopher. But to omit the punishment of a crime - for that is what 'pardoning' amounts to - even if it is endurable in other cases, is mischievous in a war like this. For there has been no civil war, of all that have occurred in the state within my memory, in which there was not certain to be some form of constitution remaining, whichever of the two sides prevailed. In this war, if we are victorious, I should not find it easy to affirm what kind of constitution we are likely to have; if we are conquered, there will certainly never be any. I therefore proposed severe measures against Antony, and severe ones also against Lepidus, and not so much out of revenge as in order that I might for the present prevent unprincipled men by this terror from attacking their country, and might for the future establish a warning for all who were minded to imitate their infatuation.

APPENDIX 2

Extract from the Roman History of Dio Cassius (AD 150-235), Volume 3, Chapter 45, Sections 17-47: an account of Cicero's public haranguing of Antony

For three men were in power - I mean Caesar and Lepidus and Antony - and of them Caesar subsequently secured the victory. At the same time that these things occurred all sorts of oracles tending to the downfall of the democracy were recited. Crows, moreover, flew into the temple of the Dioscuri and pecked out the names of the consuls and of Antony and of Dolabella, which were inscribed there somewhere on a tablet. And by night dogs in large numbers gathered throughout the city and especially near the house of the high priest, Lepidus, and set up howls. Again, the Po, which had flooded a large portion of the surrounding territory, suddenly receded and left behind on the dry land a vast number of snakes. Countless fish were cast up from the sea on the shore near the mouth of the Tiber. Succeeding these terrors a plague spread over nearly the whole of Italy in a malignant form, and in view of this the senate voted that the Curia Hostilia (one of the senate houses of the Roman Republic) should be rebuilt and the spot where the naval battle had taken place be filled up. However, the curse did not appear disposed to rest even at this point, especially when during Vibius' conduct of the initial sacrifices on the first of the month one of his lictors suddenly fell down and died. Because of these events many men in the course of those days took one side or the other in their speeches and advice, and among the deliverances was the following, of Cicero:

'You have heard recently, Conscript Fathers (that is, 'esteemed legislators'), when I made a statement to you about the matter, why I made preparations for my departure as if I were going to be absent from the city a very long time and then returned rapidly with the idea that I could benefit you greatly. I would not endure an existence under a sovereignty or a tyranny, since under such forms of government I can not enjoy the rights of free citizenship nor speak my mind safely nor die in a way that is of service to you; and again, if opportunity is afforded to obey any of duty's calls, I would not shrink from action, though it involved danger. I deem it the task of an upright man equally to keep watch over himself for his country's interests (guarding himself that he may not perish uselessly), and in this course of action not to fail to say or do whatever is requisite, even if it be necessary to suffer some harm in preserving his native land.

These assumptions granted, a large degree of safety was afforded by Caesar both to you and to me for the discussion of pressing questions. And since you have further voted to assemble under guard, we must frame all our words and behaviour this day in such a fashion as to establish the present state of affairs and provide for the future, that we may not again be compelled to decide in a similar way about it. That our condition is difficult and dangerous and requires much care and attention you yourselves have made evident, if in no other way, at least by this measure. For you would not have voted to keep the senate-house under guard, if it had been possible for you to deliberate at all with your accustomed orderliness, and in quiet, free from fear. It is necessary for us even on account of the presence of the soldiers to accomplish some measure of importance, that we may not incur the disgrace that would certainly follow from asking for them as if we feared somebody, and then neglecting affairs as if we were liable to no danger. We shall appear to have acquired them only nominally in behalf of the city against Antony, but to have given them in reality to him against our own selves, and it will look as if in addition to the other legions which he gathers against his country he needed to acquire these very men and so prevent your passing any vote against him even to-day.

Yet some have attained such a height of shamelessness as to dare to say that he is not warring against the State and have credited you with such great folly as to think that they will persuade you to attend to their words rather than to his acts. But who would choose to desist from regarding his performances and the campaign which he has made against our allies without any orders from the senate or the people, the countries which he is overrunning, the cities which he is besieging, and the hopes upon which he is building in his entire course - who would distrust, I say, the evidence of his own eyes, and to his ruin yield credence to the words of these men and their false statements, by which they put you off with pretexts and excuses?

I myself am far from asserting that in doing this he is carrying out any legal act of administration. On the contrary, because he has abandoned the province of Macedonia, which was assigned to him by lot, and because he chose instead the province of Gaul, which in no way pertained to him, and because he assumed control of the legions which Caesar had sent ahead against the Parthians, keeping them about him though no danger threatens Italy, and because he has left the city during the period of his consulship to go about pillaging and injuring the country - for all these reasons I declare that he has long been an enemy of us all. If you did not perceive it immediately at the start or experience vexation at each of his actions, he deserves to be hated all the more on this account, in that he does not cease injuring you, who are so long-suffering. He might perchance have obtained pardon for the errors which he committed at first, but now by his perseverance in evil he has reached such a pitch of knavery that he ought to be brought to book for his former offences as well. And you ought to be especially careful in regard to the situation, noticing and considering this point - that the man who has so often despised you in such weighty matters cannot submit to be corrected by the same gentleness and kindliness that you have shown, but must now against his will, even though never previously, be chastised by force of arms.

And because he partly persuaded and partly compelled you to vote him some privileges, do not think that this makes him less guilty or deserving of less punishment. Quite the reverse - for this very procedure in particular he merits the infliction of a penalty: he determined from the outset to commit many outrages, and after accomplishing some of them through you, he employed against your own selves the resources which came from you, which by deception, he forced you to vote to him, though you neither knew nor foresaw any such result. On what occasion did you voluntarily abolish the commands given by Caesar or by the lot to each man, and allow this person to distribute many appointments to his friends and companions, sending his brother Gaius to Macedonia, and assigning Gaul to himself with the aid of the legions which he was not by any means keeping to use in your defence? Do you not remember how, when he found you startled at Caesar's demise, he carried out all the plans that he chose, communicating some to you carefully dissimulated and at inopportune moments, and on his own responsibility executing others that inflicted injuries, while all his acts were characterised by violence? He used soldiers, and barbarians at that, against you. And need any one be surprised that in those days some vote was passed which should not have been, when even now we have not obtained a free hand to speak and do what is requisite in any other way than by the aid of a body-guard? If we had been formerly endued with this power, he would not have obtained what any one may say he has obtained, nor would he have risen to the prominence enabling him to do the deeds that were a natural sequence. Accordingly, let no one retort that the rights which we were seen to give him under command and compulsion and amid laments were legally and rightfully bestowed. For, even in private business, that is not considered binding which a man does under compulsion from another.

And yet all these measures which you are seen to have voted you will find to be slight and varying but little from established custom. What was there dreadful in the fact that one man was destined to govern Macedonia or Gaul in place of another? Or what was the harm if a man obtained soldiers during his consulship? But these are the facts that are harmful and abominable - that your land should be damaged, allied cities besieged, that our soldiers should be armed against us and our means expended to our detriment: this you neither voted nor intended. Do not, merely because you have granted him some privileges, allow him to usurp what was not granted him; and do not think that just as you have conceded some points he ought similarly to be permitted to do what has not been conceded. Quite the reverse: you should for this very reason both hate and punish him, because he has dared not only in this case but in all other cases to use the honour and kindness that you bestowed against you. Look at the matter. Through my influence you voted that there should be peace and harmony between individuals. This man was ordered to manage the business, and conducted it in such a way (taking Caesar's funeral as a pretext) that almost the whole city was burned down and great numbers were once more slaughtered. You ratified all the grants made to various persons and all the laws laid down by Caesar, not because they were all excellent - far from it! - but because our mutual and unsuspecting association, quite free from any disguise, was not furthered by changing any one of those enactments. This man, appointed to examine into them, has abolished many of his acts and has substituted many others in the documents. He has taken away lands and citizenship and exemption from taxes and many other honours from the possessors - private individuals, kings, and cities - and has given them to men who had not received any, altering the memoranda of Caesar; from those who were unwilling to give up anything to his grasp he took away even what had been given them, and sold this and everything else to such as wished to buy. Yet you, foreseeing this very possibility, had voted that no tablet should be set up after Caesar's death which might contain any article given by him to any person. Notwithstanding, it happened many times after that. He also said it was necessary for some provisions found in Caesar's papers to be specially noted and put into effect. You then assigned to him, in company with the foremost men, the task of making these excerpts; but he, paying no attention to his colleagues, carried out everything alone according to his wishes, in regard to the laws, the exiles, and other points which I enumerated a few moments since. This is the way in which he wishes to execute all your decrees.

Has he then shown himself such a character only in these affairs, while managing the rest rightly? In what instance? On what motive? He was ordered to search for and declare the public money left behind by Caesar, and did he not seize it, paying some of it to his creditors and spending some on high living so that he no longer has even any of this left? You hated the name of dictator on account of Caesar's sovereignty and rejected it entirely from the constitution: but is it not true that Antony, though he has avoided adopting it (as if the name in itself could do any harm), has exhibited the behaviour belonging to it and the greed for gain, under the title of consulship? You assigned to him the duty of promoting harmony, and has he not on his own responsibility begun this great war, neither necessary nor sanctioned, against Caesar and Decimus, whom you approve? Innumerable cases might be mentioned, if one wished to go into details, in which you entrusted business to him to manage as consul, and he has not conducted a single bit of it as the circumstances demanded, but has done quite the opposite, using against you the authority that you imparted. Now will you assume to yourself also these errors that he has committed and say that you yourselves are responsible for all that has happened, because you assigned to him the management and investigation of the matters in question? It is ridiculous. If some general or envoy that had been chosen should fail in every way to do his duty, you who sent him would not incur the blame for this. It would be a sorry state of things, if all who are elected to perform some work should themselves receive the advantages and the honours, but lay upon you the complaints and the blame. Accordingly, there is no sense in paying any heed to him when he says: 'It was you who permitted me to govern Gaul, you ordered me to administer the public finances, you gave me the legions from Macedonia.' Perhaps these measures were voted - yet ought you to put it that way, and not instead exact punishment from him for his action in compelling you to make that decision? At any rate, you never at any time gave him the right to restore the exiles, to add laws surreptitiously, to sell the privileges of citizenship and exemption from taxes, to steal the public funds, to plunder the possessions of allies, to abuse the cities, or to undertake to play the tyrant over his native country. And you never conceded to any one else all that was desired, though you have granted by your votes many things to many persons; on the contrary you have always punished such men so far as you could, as you will also punish him, if you take my advice. For it is not in these matters alone that he has shown himself to be such a man as you know and have seen him to be, but briefly in all undertakings which he has ever attempted to perform for the commonwealth.

His private life and his private examples of licentiousness and avarice I shall willingly pass over, not because one would fail to discover that he had committed many abominable outrages in the course of them, but because, by Hercules, I am ashamed to describe minutely and separately - especially to you who know it as well as I - how he conducted his youth among you who were boys at the time, how he auctioned off the vigour of his prime, his secret lapses from chastity, his open fornications, what he let be done to him as long as it was possible, what he did as early as he could, his revels, his periods of drunkenness, and all the rest that follows in their train. It is impossible for a person brought up in so great licentiousness and shamelessness to avoid defiling his entire life: and so from his private concerns he brought his lewdness and greed to bear upon public matters. On this I will refrain from dilating, and likewise by Jupiter on his visit to Gabinius in Egypt and his flight to Caesar in Gaul, that I may not be charged with going minutely into every detail; for I feel ashamed for you, that knowing him to be such a man you appointed him tribune and master of the horse and subsequently consul. I will at present recite only his drunken insolence and abuses in these very positions.

Well, then, when he was tribune he first of all prevented you from settling suitably the work you then had in hand by shouting and bawling and alone of all the people opposing the public peace of the State, until you became vexed and because of his conduct passed the vote that you did. Then, though by law he was not permitted to be absent from town a single night, he escaped from the city, abandoning the duties of his office, and, having gone as a deserter to Caesar's camp, guided the latter back as a foe to his country, drove you out of Rome and all the rest of Italy, and, in short, became the prime cause of all the civil disorders that have since taken place among you. Had he not at that time acted contrary to your wishes, Caesar would never have found an excuse for the war and could not, in spite of all his shamelessness, have gathered a competent force in defiance of your resolutions; but he would have either voluntarily laid down his arms, or been brought to his senses unwillingly. As it is, this fellow is the man who furnished him with the excuses, who destroyed the prestige of the senate, who increased the audacity of the soldiers. He it is who planted the seeds of evils which sprang up afterward: he it is who has proved the common bane not only of us, but also of practically the whole world, as, indeed, Heaven rather plainly indicated. When, that is to say, he proposed those astonishing laws, the whole air was filled with thunder and lightning. Yet this accursed wretch paid no attention to them, though he claims to be a soothsayer, but filled not only the city but the whole world with the evils and wars which I mentioned.

Now after this is there any need of mentioning that he served as master of the horse an entire year, something which had never before been done? Or that during this period also he was drunk and abusive and in the assemblies would frequently vomit the remains of yesterday's debauch on the rostra itself, in the midst of his harangues? Or that he went about Italy at the head of pimps and prostitutes and buffoons, women as well as men, in company with the lictors bearing festoons of laurel? Or that he alone of mankind dared to buy the property of Pompey, having no regard for his own dignity or the great man's memory, but grasping eagerly those possessions over which we even now as at that time shed a tear? He threw himself upon this and many other estates with the evident intention of making no recompense for them. Yet with all his insolence and violence the price was nevertheless collected, for Caesar took this way of discountenancing his act. And all that he has acquired, vast in extent and gathered from every source, he has consumed in dicing, consumed in harlotry, consumed in feasting, consumed in drinking, like a second Charybdis.

Of this behaviour I shall make no chronicle. But on the subject of the insults which he offered to the State and the assassinations which he caused throughout the whole city alike how can any man be silent? Is memory lacking of how oppressive the very sight of him was to you, but most of all his deeds? He dared, O thou earth and ye gods, first in this place, within the wall, in the Forum, in the senate-house, on the Capitol, at one and the same time to array himself in the purple-bordered garb, to gird a sword on his thigh, to employ lictors, and to be escorted by armed soldiers. Next, whereas he might have checked the turmoil of the citizens, he not only failed to do so, but set you at variance when you were in concord, partly by his own acts and partly through the medium of others. Moreover he directed his attention in turn to the latter themselves, and by now assisting them and now abandoning them incurred full responsibility for great numbers of them being slain and for the fact that the entire region of Pontus and of the Parthians was not subdued at that time immediately after the victory over Pharnaces. Caesar, being called hither in haste to see what he was doing, did not finish entirely any of those projects, as he was surely intending.

Even this result did not sober him, but when he was consul he came naked, naked, Conscript Fathers, and anointed into the Forum, taking the Lupercalia as an excuse, then proceeded in company with his lictors to the rostra, and there harangued us from the elevation. From the day the city was founded no one can point to any one else, even a praetor or tribune or aedile, let alone a consul, who has done such a thing. To be sure it was the festival of the Lupercalia, and the Lupercalia had been put in charge of the Julian College; yes, and Sextus Clodius had trained him to conduct himself so, upon receipt of two thousand plethra of the land of Leontini. But you were consul, respected sir (for I will address you as though you were present), and it was neither proper nor permissible for you as such to speak in such a way in the Forum, hard by the rostra, with all of us present, and to cause us both to behold your remarkable body, so corpulent and detestable, and to hear your accursed voice, choked with unguent, speaking those outrageous words; for I will preferably confine my comment to this point about your mouth. The Lupercalia would not have missed its proper reverence, but you disgraced the whole city at once - not to speak a word yet about your remarks on that occasion. Who is unaware that the consulship is public, the property of the whole people, that its dignity must be preserved everywhere, and that its holder must nowhere strip naked or behave wantonly? Did he perchance imitate the famous Horatius of old or Cloelia of bygone days? But the latter swam across the river with all her clothing, and the former cast himself with his armour into the flood. It would be fitting - would it not? - to set up also a statue of this consul, so that people might contrast the one man armed in the Tiber and the other naked in the Forum. It was by such conduct as has been cited that those heroes of yore were wont to preserve us and give us liberty, while he took away all our liberty from us, so far as was in his power, destroyed the whole democracy, set up a despot in place of a consul, a tyrant in place of a dictator over us. You remember the nature of his language when he approached the rostra, and the style of his behaviour when he had ascended it. But when a man who is a Roman and a consul has dared to name any one King of the Romans in the Roman Forum, close to the rostra of liberty, in the presence of the entire people and the entire senate, and straightway to set the diadem upon his head and further to affirm falsely in the hearing of us all that we ourselves bade him say and do this, what most outrageous deed will that man not dare, and from what action, however revolting, will he refrain? Did we lay this injunction upon you, Antony, we who expelled the Tarquins, who cherished Brutus, who hurled Capitolinus headlong, who put to death the Spurii? Did we order you to salute any one as king, when we have laid a curse upon the very name of monarch and furthermore upon that of dictator as the most similar? Did we command you to appoint any one tyrant, we who repulsed Pyrrhus from Italy, who drove back Antiochus beyond the Taurus, who put an end to the tyranny even in Macedonia? No, by the rods of Valerius and the law of Porcius, no, by the leg of Horatius and the hand of Mucius, no, by the spear of Decius and the sword of Brutus! But you, unspeakable villain, begged and pleaded to be made a slave as Postumius pleaded to be delivered to the Samnites, as Regulus to be given back to the Carthaginians, as Curtius to be thrown into the chasm. And where did you find this recorded? In the same place where you discovered that the Cretans had been made free after Brutus was their governor, when we voted after Caesar's death that he should govern them.

So then, seeing that you have detected his baneful disposition in so many and so great enterprises, will you not take vengeance on him instead of waiting to learn by experience what the man who caused so much trouble naked will do to you when he is armed? Do you think that he is not eager for the tyrant's power, that he does not pray to obtain it some day, or that he will put the pursuit of it out of his thoughts, when he has once allowed it a resting-place in his mind, and that he will ever abandon the hope of sole rulership for which he has spoken and acted so impudently without punishment! What human being who, while master of his own voice, would undertake to help some one else secure an honour, would not appropriate it himself when he became powerful? Who that has dared to nominate another as tyrant over his country and himself at once would himself refuse to be monarch? Hence, even if you spared him formerly, you must hate him now for these acts. Do not desire to learn what he will do when his success equals his wishes, but on the basis of his previous ventures plan beforehand to suffer no further outrages. What defence could anyone make of what took place? That Caesar acted rightly at that time in accepting neither the name of king nor the diadem? If so, this man did wrong to offer something which pleased not even Caesar. Or, on the other hand, that the latter erred in enduring at all to look on at and listen to such proceedings? If so, and Caesar justly suffered death for this error, does not this man, admitted in a certain way that he desired a tyranny, most richly deserve to perish? That this is so is evident from what I have previously said, but is proved most clearly by what he did after that. What other end than supremacy had he in mind that he has undertaken to cause agitation and to meddle in private business, when he might have enjoyed quiet with safety? What other end, that he has entered upon campaigns and warfare, when it was in his power to remain at home without danger? For what reason, when many have disliked to go out and take charge even of the offices that belonged to them, does he not only lay claim to Gaul, which pertains to him in not the slightest degree, but use force upon it because of its unwillingness? For what reason, when Decimus Brutus is ready to surrender to us himself and his soldiers and the cities, has this man not imitated him, instead of besieging and shutting him up? The only interpretation to be put upon it is that he is strengthening himself in this and every other way against us, and to no other end.

Seeing this, do we delay and give way to weakness and train up so monstrous a tyrant against our own selves? Is it not disgraceful that our forefathers, brought up in slavery, felt the desire for liberty, but we who have lived under an independent government become slaves of our own free will? Or again, that we were glad to rid ourselves of the dominion of Caesar, though we had first received many favours from his hands, and accept in his stead this man, a self-elected despot, who is far worse than he; this allegation is proved by the fact that Caesar spared many after his victories in war, but this follower of his before attaining any power has slaughtered three hundred soldiers, among them some centurions, guilty of no wrong, at home, in his own quarters, before the face and eyes of his wife, so that she too was defiled with blood. What do you think that the man who treated them so cruelly, when he owed them care, will refrain from doing to all of you - aye, down to the utmost outrage - if he shall conquer? And how can you believe that the man who has lived so licentiously even to the present time will not proceed to all extremes of wantonness, if he shall further secure the authority given by arms?

Do not, then, wait until you have suffered some such treatment and begin to rue it, but guard yourselves before you are molested. It is out of the question to allow dangers to come upon you and then repent of it, when you might have anticipated them. And do not choose to neglect the seriousness of the present situation and then ask again for another Cassius or some more Brutuses. It is ridiculous, when we have the power of aiding ourselves in time, to seek later on men to set us free. Perhaps we should not even find them, especially if we handle in such a way the present situation. Who would privately choose to run risks for the democracy, when he sees that we are publicly resigned to slavery? It must be evident to every man that Antony will not rest contented with what he is now doing, but that in far off and small concerns even he is strengthening himself against us. He is warring against Decimus and besieging Mutina for no other purpose than to provide himself, by conquering and capturing them, with resources against us. He has not been wronged by them that he can appear to be defending himself, nor does he merely desire the property that they possess and with this in mind endure toils and dangers, while ready and willing to relinquish that belonging to us, who own their property and much beside. Shall we wait for him to secure the prize and still more, and so become a dangerous foe? Shall we trust his deception when he says that he is not warring against the City? Who is so silly as to decide whether a man is making war on us or not by his words rather than by his deeds? I do not say that now for the first time is he unfriendly to us, when he has abandoned the City and made a campaign against allies and is assailing Brutus and besieging the cities; but on the basis of his former evil and licentious behaviour, not only after Caesar's death but even in the latter's lifetime, I decide that he has shown himself an enemy of our government and liberty and a plotter against them. Who that loved his country or hated tyranny would have committed a single one of the many and manifold offences laid to this man's charge? From every point of view he is proved to have long been an enemy of ours, and the case stands as follows. If we now take measures against him with all speed, we shall get back all that has been lost: but if, neglecting to do this, we wait till he himself admits that he is plotting against us, we shall lose everything. This he will never do, not even if he should actually march upon the City, any more than Marius or Cinna or Sulla did. But if he gets control of affairs, he will not fail to act precisely as they did, or still worse. Men who are anxious to accomplish an object are wont to say one thing, and those who have succeeded in accomplishing it are wont to do quite a different thing. To gain their end they pretend anything, but having obtained it they deny themselves the gratification of no desire. Furthermore, the last born always desire to surpass what their predecessors have ventured: they think it a small thing to behave like them and do something that has been effected before, but determine that something original is the only thing worthy of them, because unexpected.

Seeing this, then, Conscript Fathers, let us no longer delay nor fall a prey to the indolence that the moment inspires, but

decided wrongly and ought to submit to punishment, because without our sanction or that of the people they have dared to offer armed resistance to their consul, some having deserted his standard, and others having been gathered against him. The other is to say that Antony by reason of his deeds has in our judgment long since admitted that he is our enemy and by public consent ought to be chastised by us all. No one can be ignorant that the latter decision is not only more just but more expedient for us. The man neither understands how to handle business himself (how or by what means could a person that lives in drunkenness and dicing?) nor has he any companion who is of any account. He loves only such as are like himself and makes them the confidants of all his open and secret undertakings. Also he is most cowardly in extreme dangers and most treacherous even to his intimate friends, neither of which qualities is suited for generalship or war. Who can be unaware that this very man caused all our internal troubles and then shared the dangers to the slightest possible degree? He tarried long in Brundusium through cowardice, so that Caesar was isolated and on account of him almost failed: likewise he held aloof from all succeeding wars - that against the Egyptians, against Pharnaces, the African, and the Spanish. Who is unaware that he won the favour of Clodius, and after using the latter's tribuneship for the most outrageous ends would have killed him with his own hand, if I had accepted this promise from him? Again, in the matter of Caesar, he was first associated with him as quaestor, when Caesar was praetor in Spain, next attached himself to him during the tribuneship, contrary to the liking of us all, and later received from him countless money and excessive honours: in return for this he tried to inspire his patron with a desire for supremacy, which led to talk against him and was more than anything else responsible for Caesar's death.

Yet he once stated that it was I who directed the assassins to their work. He is so senseless as to venture to invent so great praise for me. And I for my part do not affirm that he was the actual slayer of Caesar - not because he was not willing, but because in this, too, he was timid - yet by the very course of his actions I say that Caesar perished at his hands. For this is the man who provided a motive, so that there seemed to be some justice in plotting against him, this is he who called him 'king', who gave him the diadem, who previously slandered him actually to his friends. Do I rejoice at the death of Caesar, I, who never enjoyed anything but liberty at his hands, and is Antony grieved, who has rapaciously seized his whole property and committed many injuries on the pretext of his letters, and is finally hastening to succeed to his position of ruler?

But I return to the point that he has none of the qualities of a great general or such as to bring victory, and does not possess many or formidable forces. The majority of the soldiers and the best ones have abandoned him to his fate, and also, by Jupiter, he has been deprived of the elephants. The remainder have perfected themselves rather in outraging and pillaging the possessions of the allies than in waging war, A proof of the sort of spirit that animates them lies in the fact that they still adhere to him, and of their lack of fortitude in that they have not taken Mutina, though they have now been besieging it for so long a time. Such is the condition of Antony and of his followers found to be. But Caesar and Brutus and those arrayed with them are firmly intrenched without outside aid; Caesar, in fact, has won over many of his rival's soldiers, and Brutus is keeping the same usurper out of Gaul: and if you come to their assistance, first by approving what they have done of their own motion, next by ratifying their acts, at the same time giving them legal authority for the future, and next by sending out both the consuls to take charge of the war, it is not possible that any of his present associates will continue to aid him. However, even if they should cling to him most tenaciously, they would not he able to resist all the rest at once, but he will either lay down his arms voluntarily, as soon as he ascertains that you have passed this vote, and place himself in your hands, or he will be captured involuntarily as the result of one battle.

I give you this advice, and, if it had been my lot to be consul, I should have certainly carried it out, as I did in former days when I defended you against Catiline and Lentulus (a relative of this very man), who had formed a conspiracy. Perhaps some one of you regards these statements as well put, but thinks we ought first to despatch envoys to him, then, after learning his decision, in case he will voluntarily give up his arms and submit himself to you, to take no action, but if he sticks to the same principles, then to declare war upon him: this is the advice which I hear some persons wish to give you. This policy is very attractive in theory, but in fact it is disgraceful and dangerous to the city. Is it not disgraceful that you should employ heralds and embassies to citizens?

With foreign nations it is proper and necessary to treat by heralds in advance, but upon citizens who are at all guilty you should inflict punishment straightway, by trying them in court if you can get them under the power of your votes, and by warring against them if you find them in arms. All such are slaves of you and of the people and of the laws, whether they wish it or not; and it is not fitting either to coddle them or to put them on an equal footing with the highest class of free persons, but to pursue and chastise them like runaway servants, with a feeling of your own superiority. Is it not a disgrace that he should not delay to wrong us, but we delay to defend ourselves? Or again, that he should for a long time, weapons in hand, have been carrying on the entire practice of war, while we waste time in decrees and embassies, and that we should retaliate only with letters and phrases upon the man whom we have long since discovered by his deeds to be a wrongdoer? What do we expect? That he will some day render us obedience and pay us respect? How can this prove true of a man who has come into such a condition that he would not be able, even should he wish it, to be an ordinary citizen with you under a democratic government? If he were willing to conduct his life on fair and equitable principles, he would never have entered in the first place upon such a career as his: and if he had done it under the influence of folly or recklessness, he would certainly have given it up speedily of his own accord. As the case stands, since he has once overstepped the limits imposed by the laws and the government and has acquired some power and authority by this action, it is not conceivable that he would change of his own free will or heed any one of our resolutions, but it is absolutely requisite that such a man should be chastised with those very weapons with which he has dared to wrong us. And I beg you now to remember particularly a sentence which this man himself once uttered, that it is impossible for you to be saved, unless you conquer. Hence those who bid you send envoys are doing nothing else than planning how you may be dilatory and the body of your allies become as a consequence more feeble and dispirited; while he, on the other hand, will be doing whatever he pleases, will destroy Decimus, storm Mutina, and capture all of Gaul: the result will be that we can no longer find means to deal with him, but shall be under the necessity of trembling before him, paying court to him, worshiping him. This one thing more about the embassy and I am done - that Antony also gave you no account of what business he had in hand, because he intended that you should do this.

I, therefore, for these and all other reasons advise you not to delay nor to lose time, but to make war upon him as quickly as possible. You must reflect that the majority of enterprises owe their success rather to an opportune occasion than to their strength; and you should by all means feel perfectly sure that I would never give up peace if it were really peace, in the midst of which I have most influence and have acquired wealth and reputation, nor have urged you to make war, did I not think it to your advantage.

And I advise you, Calenus, and the rest who are of the same mind as you, to be quiet and allow the senate to vote the requisite measures and not for the sake of your private good-will toward Antony recklessly betray the common interests of all of us. Indeed, I am of the opinion, Conscript Fathers, that if you heed my counsel I may enjoy in your company and with thorough satisfaction freedom and preservation, but that if you vote anything different, I shall choose to die rather than to live. I have, in general, never been afraid of death as a consequence of my outspokenness, and now I fear it least of all. That accounts, indeed, for my overwhelming success, the proof of which lies in the fact that you decreed a sacrifice and festival in memory of the deeds done in my consulship - an honour which had never before been granted to anyone, even to one who had achieved some great end in war. Death, if it befell me, would not be at all unseasonable, especially when you consider that my consulship was so many years ago; yet remember that in that very consulship I uttered the same sentiment, to make you feel that in any and all business I despised death. To dread any one, however, that was against you, and in your company to be a slave to anyone would prove exceedingly unseasonable to me. Wherefore I deem this last to be the ruin and destruction not only of the body, but of the soul and reputation, by which we become in a certain sense immortal. But to die speaking and acting in your behalf I regard as equivalent to immortality.

And if Antony, also, felt the force of this, he would never have entered upon such a career, but would have even preferred to die like his grandfather rather than to behave like Cinna who killed him. For, putting aside other considerations, Cinna was in turn slain not long afterward for this and the other sins that he had committed; so that I am surprised also at this feature in Antony's conduct, that, imitating his works as he does, he shows no fear of some day falling a victim to a similar disaster: the murdered man, however, left behind to this very descendant the reputation of greatness. But the latter has no longer any claim to be saved on account of his relatives, since he has neither emulated his grandfather nor inherited his father's property. Who is unaware of the fact that in restoring many who were exiled in Caesar's time and later, in accordance forsooth with directions in his patron's papers, he did not aid his uncle, but brought back his fellow-gambler Lenticulus, who was exiled for his unprincipled life, and cherishes Bambalio, who is notorious for his very name, while he has treated his nearest relatives as I have described and as if he were half angry at them because he was born into that family. Consequently he never inherited his father's goods, but has been the heir of very many others, some whom he never saw or heard of, and others who are still living. That is, he has so stripped and despoiled them that they differ in no way from dead men.'

APPENDIX 3

Extract from the Roman History of Dio Cassius
(AD 150-235), Volume 3, Chapter 46, Sections 48 onwards:
the reply to Cicero's accusations made by the general,
Quintus Fufius Calenus, Antony's friend and supporter

When Cicero had finished speaking in this vein, Quintus
Fufius Calenus (a general and a supporter of Antony) arose
and said:

'Ordinarily I should not have wished either to say anything
in defence of Antony or to assail Cicero. I really do not think
it proper in such discussions as is the present to do either of
these things, but simply to make known what one's opinion
is. The former method belongs to the courtroom, whereas
this is a matter of deliberation. Since, however, he has
undertaken to speak ill of Antony on account of the enmity
that exists between them, instead of sending him a summons,
as he ought, if Antony were guilty of any wrong, and since

he has further mentioned me in a calumnious fashion, as if he could not have exhibited his cleverness without heedlessly insulting one or two persons, it behooves me also to set aside the imputation against Antony and to bring counter-charges against the speaker. I would not have his innate impudence fail of a response nor let my silence aid him by incurring the suspicion of a guilty conscience; nor would I have you, deceived by what he said, come to a less worthy decision by accepting his private spleen against Antony in exchange for the common advantage. He wishes to effect nothing else than that we should abandon looking out for the safest course for the commonwealth and fall into discord again. It is not the first time that he has done this, but from the outset, ever since he had to do with politics, he has been continually causing disturbance one way or the other.

Is he not the one who embroiled Caesar with Pompey and prevented Pompey from becoming reconciled with Caesar? The one who persuaded you to pass that vote against Antony by which he irritated Caesar, and persuaded Pompey to leave Italy and transfer his quarters to Macedonìa? This proved the chief cause of all the evils which befell us subsequently. Is not he the one who killed Clodius by the hand of Milo, and slew Caesar by the hand of Brutus? The one who made Catiline hostile to us and despatched Lentulus without a trial? Hence I should be very much surprised at you, seeing that you then changed your mind about his conduct just mentioned and made him pay the penalty for it, if you should now heed him again, when his talk and actions are similar. Do you not see, too, that after Caesar's death when our affairs were settled in a most tranquil way by Antony, as not even his accuser can deny, the latter left town because he deemed our life of harmony to be alien and dangerous to him? That when he perceived that turmoil had again arisen, he bade a long farewell to his son and to Athens, and returned? That he insults and abuses Antony, whom he was wont to say he loved, and cooperates with Caesar, whose father he killed? And if chance so favour, he will ere long attack Caesar also. For the fellow is naturally distrustful and turbulent and has no ballast in his soul, and he is always stirring things up and twisting about, turning more ways than the sea-passage to which he fled and got the title of deserter for it, asking all of you to take that man for friend or foe whom he bids.

For these reasons be on your guard against this man. He is a juggler and imposter and grows rich and strong from the ills of others, blackmailing, dragging, tearing the innocent, as do dogs; but in the midst of public harmony he is embarrassed and withers away. It is not friendship or good-will among us that can support this kind of orator. From what other source do you think he has become rich or from what other source great? Certainly neither family nor wealth was bequeathed him by his father the fuller, who was always trading in grapes and olives, a man who was glad to make both ends meet by this and by his washing, and whose time was taken up every day and night with the vilest occupations. The son, having been brought up in them, not unnaturally tramples and dowses his superiors, using a species of abuse invented in the workshops and on the street corners.

Now being of such an origin yourself, and after growing up naked among your naked companions, picking up pig manure and sheep dung and human excrement, have you dared, O most accursed wretch, first to slander the youth of Antony who had the advantage of pedagogues and teachers as his rank demanded, and next to impugn him because in celebrating the Lupercalia, an ancestral festival, he came naked into the Forum? But I ask you, you that always used all the clothes of others on account of your father's business and were stripped by whoever met you and recognised them, what ought a man who was not only priest but also leader of his fellow priests to have done? Not to conduct the procession, not to celebrate the festival, not to sacrifice according to ancestral custom, not to appear naked, not to anoint himself? 'But it is not for that that I censure him,' he answers, 'but because he delivered a speech and that kind of speech naked in the Forum.' Of course this man has become acquainted in the fuller's shop with all minute matters of etiquette, that he should detect a real mistake and be able to rebuke it properly.

In regard to this matter I will say later all that needs to be said, but just now I want to ask the speaker a question or two. Is it not true that you for your part were nourished by the ills of others and educated in the misfortunes of your neighbours and for this reason are acquainted with no liberal branch of knowledge, that you have established a kind of association here and are always waiting, like the harlots, for a man who will give something, and that having many men in your pay to attract profit to you, you pry into people's affairs to find out who has wronged (or seems to have wronged) whom, who hates whom, and who is plotting against whom? With these men you make common cause, and through these men you are supported, selling them the hopes that chance bestows, trading in the decisions of the jurors, deeming him alone a friend who gives more and more, and all those enemies who furnish you no business or employ some other advocate, while you pretend not even to know those who are already in your clutch and affect to be bored by them, but fawn upon and giggle at those just approaching, like the mistresses of inns?

How much better it were that you too should have been born Bambalio - if this Bambalio really exists - than to have taken up such a livelihood, in which it is absolutely inevitable that you should either sell your speech in behalf of the innocent, or else preserve the guilty. Yet you cannot do even this effectively, though you wasted three years in Athens. On what occasion? By what help? Why, you always come trembling up to court as if you were going to fight in armour and after speaking a few words in a low and half-dead voice you go away, not remembering a word of the speech you practised at home before you came, and without finding anything to say on the spur of the moment. In making affirmations and promises you surpass all mankind in audacity, but in the contests themselves beyond uttering some words of abuse and defamation you are most weak and cowardly. Do you think any one is ignorant of the fact that you never delivered one of those wonderful speeches of yours that you have published, but wrote them all up afterward, like persons who form generals and masters-of-horse out of day? If you feel doubtful of this point, remember how you accused Verres - though, to be sure, you only gave him an example of your father's trade, when you made water.

But I hesitate, for fear that in saying precisely what fits your case I may seem to be uttering words that are unfitting for myself. This I will pass over; and further, by Jupiter, also the affairs of Gabinius, against whom you prepared accusers and then pled his cause in such a way that he was condemned; and the pamphlets which you compose against your friends, in regard to which you feel yourself so guilty that you do not dare to make them public. Yet it is a most miserable and pitiable state to be in, not to be able to deny these charges which are the most disgraceful conceivable to admit. But I will leave these to one side and bring forward the rest. Well, though we did grant the trainer, as you say, two thousand plethra of the auger Leontinus, we still learned nothing adequate from it. But who should not admire your system of instruction? And what is it? You are ever jealous of your superiors, you always toady to the prominent man, you slander him who has attained distinction, you inform against the powerful and you hate equally all the excellent, and you pretend love only for those through whom you may do some mischief. This is why you are always inciting the younger against their elders and lead those who trust you even in the slightest into dangers, where you desert them. A proof of this is, that you have never accomplished any achievement worthy of a distinguished man either in war or in peace. How many wars have we won under you as praetor and what kind of territory did we acquire with you as consul? Your private activity all these years has consisted in continually deceiving some of the foremost men and winning them to your side and managing everything you like, while publicly you have been shouting and bawling out at random those detestable phrases - 'I am the only one that loves you,' or, if it should so chance, 'And what's-his-name, all the rest, hate you,' and 'I alone am friendly to you, all the rest are engaged in plots,' and other such stuff by which you fill some with elation and conceit, only to betray them, and scare the rest so that you gain their attachment. If any service is rendered by any one whomsoever of the whole people, you lay claim to it and write your own name upon it, repeating, 'I moved it, I proposed it, it was through me that this was done so'. But if anything happens that ought not to have occurred, you take yourself out of the way and censure all the rest, saying, 'You see I wasn't praetor, you see I wasn't envoy, you see I wasn't consul.' And you abuse everybody everywhere all the time, setting more store by the influence which comes from appearing to speak your mind boldly than by saying what duty demands: and you exhibit no important quality of an orator. What public advantage has been preserved or established by you? Who that was really harming the city have you indicted, and who that was really plotting against us have you brought to light? To neglect the other cases - these very charges which you now bring against Antony are of such a nature and so many that no one could ever suffer any adequate penalty for them. Why, then, if you saw us being wronged by him at the start, as you assert, did you never attack or accuse him at the time, instead of telling us now all the transgressions he committed when tribune, all his irregularities when master of horse, all his villainies when consul? You might at once, at the time, in each specific instance, have inflicted the appropriate penalty upon him, if you had wanted to show yourself in very deed a patriot, and we could have imposed the punishment in security and safety during the course of the offences themselves. One of two conclusions is inevitable - either that you believed this to be so at the time and renounced the idea of a struggle in our behalf, or else that you could not prove any of your charges and are now engaged in a reckless course of blackmail.

That this is so I will show you clearly, Conscript Fathers, by going over each point in detail. Antony did say some words during his tribuneship in Caesar's behalf: Cicero and some others spoke in behalf of Pompey. Why now does he accuse him of preferring one man's friendship, but acquit himself and the rest who warmly embraced the opposite cause? Antony, to be sure, hindered at that time some measures adverse to Caesar from being passed: and Cicero hindered practically everything that was known to be favourable to Caesar. 'But Antony obstructed', he replies, 'the public judgment of the senate'. Well, now, in the first place, how could one man have had so much power? Second, if he had been condemned for this, as is said, how could he have escaped punishment? 'Oh, he fled, he fled to Caesar and got out of the way'. Of course you, Cicero, did not 'leave town' just now, but you fled, as in your former exile. Don't be so ready to apply your own shame to all of us. To flee is what you did, in fear of the court, and pronouncing condemnation on yourself beforehand. Yes, to be sure, an ordinance was passed for your recall; how and for what reasons I do not say, but at any rate it was passed, and you did not set foot in Italy before the recall was granted. But Antony both went away to Caesar to inform him what had been done and returned, without asking for any decree, and finally effected peace and friendship with him for all those that were found in Italy. And the rest, too, would have had a share in it, if they had not taken your advice and fled. Now in view of those circumstances do you dare to say he led Caesar against his country and stirred up the civil war and became more than any one else responsible for the subsequent evils that befell us? Not so, but you, who gave Pompey legions that belonged to others and the command, and undertook to deprive Caesar even of those that had been given him: it was you, who agreed with Pompey and the consuls not to accept the offers made by Caesar, but to abandon the city and the whole of Italy; you, who did not see Caesar even when he entered Rome, but had run off to Pompey and into Macedonia. Not even to him, however, did you prove of any assistance, but you neglected what was going on, and then, when he met with misfortune, you abandoned him. Therefore you did not aid him at the outset on the ground that he had the juster cause, but after setting in motion the dispute and embroiling affairs you lay in wait at a safe distance for a favourable turn; you at once deserted the man who failed, as if that somehow proved him guilty, and went over to the victor, as if you deemed him more just. And in addition to your other defects you are so ungrateful that not only are you not satisfied to have been preserved by him, but you are actually displeased that you were not made master of the horse.

Then with this on your conscience do you dare to say that Antony ought not to have held the office of master of the horse for a year, and that Caesar ought not to have remained dictator for a year? But whether it was wise or necessary for these measures to be framed, at any rate they were both passed, and they suited us and the people. Censure these men, Cicero, if they have transgressed in any particular, but not, by Jupiter, those whom they have chosen to honour for showing themselves worthy of so great a reward. For if we were forced by the circumstances that then surrounded us to act in this way and contrary to good policy, why do you now lay this upon Antony's shoulders, and why did you not oppose it then if you were able? Because, by Jupiter, you were afraid. Then shall you, who were at that time silent, obtain pardon for your cowardice, and shall he, because he was preferred before you, submit to penalties for his excellence? Where did you learn that this was just, or where did you read that this was lawful?

'But he did not rightly use his position as master of horse'. Why? Because, he answers, 'he bought Pompey's possessions'. How many others are there who purchased numberless articles, no one of whom is blamed? That was the purpose in confiscating certain articles and exposing them in the market and proclaiming them by the voice of the public crier, to have somebody buy them. 'But Pompey's goods ought not to have been sold'. Then it was we who erred and did wrong in confiscating them; or (to clear your skirts and ours) it was at least Caesar who acted irregularly, he who ordered this to be done: yet you did not censure him at all. I maintain that in this charge he is proven to be absolutely beside himself. He has brought against Antony two quite opposite accusations - one, that after helping Caesar in very many ways and receiving in return vast gifts from him he was then required under compulsion to surrender the price of them, and the second, that he inherited naught from his father, spent all that he had like Charybdis (the speaker is always bringing in some comparison from Sicily, as if we had forgotten that he had been exiled there), and paid the price of all that he purchased.

So in these charges this remarkable orator is convicted of violently contradicting himself and, by Jupiter, again in the following statements. At one time he says that Antony took part in everything that was done by Caesar and by this means became more than any one else responsible for all our internal evils, and again he charges him with cowardice, reproaching him with not having shared in any other exploits than those performed in Thessaly. And he makes a complaint against him to the effect that he restored some of the exiles and finds fault with him because he did not secure the recall of his uncle; as if any one believes that he would not have restored him first of all, if he had been able to recall whomsoever he pleased, since there was no grievance on either side between them, as this speaker himself knows. Indeed, though he told many wretched lies about Antony, he did not dare to say anything of that kind. But he is utterly reckless about letting slip anything that comes to his tongue's end, as if it were mere breath.

Why should one follow this line of refutation further? Turning now to the fact that he goes about with such a tragic air, and has but this moment said in the course of his remarks that Antony rendered the sight of the master of the horse most oppressive by using everywhere and under all circumstances the sword, the purple, the lictors, and the soldiers at once, let him tell me clearly how and in what respect we have been wronged by this. He will have no statement to make; for if he had had, he would have sputtered it out before anything else. Quite the reverse of his charge is true. Those who were quarrelling at that time and causing all the trouble were Trebellius and Dolabella: Antony did no wrong and was active in every way in our behalf, so much so that he was entrusted by us with guarding the city against those very men, and not only did this remarkable orator not oppose it (he was there) but even approved it. Else let him show what syllable he uttered on seeing the licentious and accursed fellow (to quote from his abuse), besides doing nothing that the occasion required, securing also so great authority from you. He will have nothing to show. So it looks as if not a word of what he now shouts aloud was ventured at that time by this great and patriotic orator, who is everywhere and always saying and repeating, 'I alone am contending for freedom, I alone speak freely for the democracy; I cannot be restrained by favour of friends or fear of enemies from looking out for your advantage; I, even if it should be my lot to die in speaking in your behalf, will perish very gladly'. And his silence was very natural, for it occurred to him to reflect that Antony possessed the lictors and the purple-bordered vesture in accordance with the customs of our ancestors in regard to masters of horse, and that he was using the sword and the soldiers perforce against the rebels. For what most excessive outrages would they not have committed but for his being hedged about with these protections, when some of them so despised him as it was?

That these and all his other acts were correct and most thoroughly in accord with Caesar's intention the facts themselves show. The rebellion went no further, and Antony, far from paying a penalty for his course, was subsequently appointed consul. Notice, I beg of you, how he administered this office of his. You will find, if you scrutinise the matter minutely, that its tenure proved of great value to the city. His traducer, knowing this, could not endure his jealousy but dared to slander him for those deeds which he would have longed to do himself. That is why he introduced the matter of his stripping and anointing and those ancient fables, not because there was any pertinence in them now, but in order to obscure by external noise his opponent's consummate skill and success. Yet this same Antony, O thou earth, and ye gods (I shall call louder than you and invoke them with greater justice), saw that the city was already in reality under a tyranny through the fact that all the legions obeyed Caesar and all the people together with the senate submitted to him to such an extent that they voted among other measures that he should be dictator for life and use the appurtenances of a king. Then he showed Caesar his error most convincingly and restrained him most prudently, until the latter, abashed and afraid, would not accept either the name of king or the diadem, which he had in mind to bestow upon himself even against our will. Any other man would have declared that he had been ordered to do it by his master, and putting forward the compulsion as an excuse would have obtained pardon for it - yes, indeed, he would, when you think of what kind of votes we had passed at that time and what power the soldiers had secured. Antony, however, because he was thoroughly acquainted with Caesar's disposition and accurately aware of all he was preparing to do, by great good judgment succeeded in turning him aside from his course and retarding his ambitions. The proof of it is that afterward he no longer behaved in any way like a monarch, but mingled publicly and unprotected with us all; and that accounts most of all for the possibility of his meeting the fate that he did.

This is what was done, O Cicero or Cicerulus or Ciceracius or Ciceriscus or Graeculus or whatever you like to be called, by the uneducated, the naked, the anointed man: and none of it was done by you, the clever, the wise, the user of much more olive oil than wine, you who let your clothing drag about your ankles not, by Jupiter, as the dancers do, who teach you intricacies of reasoning by their poses, but in order to hide the ugliness of your legs. Oh no, it's not through modesty that you do this, you who delivered that long screed about Antony's habits. Who is there that does not see these soft clothes of yours? Who does not scent your carefully combed grey locks? Who is there unaware that you put away your first wife who had borne you two children, and at an advanced age married another, a mere girl, in order that you might pay your debts out of her property? And you did not even retain her, to the end that you might keep Caerellia fearlessly, whom you debauched when she was as much older than yourself as the maiden you married was younger, and to whom you write such letters as a jester at no loss for words would write if he were trying to get up an amour with a woman seventy years old. This, which is not altogether to my taste, I have been induced to say, Conscript Fathers, in the hope that he should not go away without getting as good as he sent in the discussion. Again, he has ventured to reproach Antony for a little kind of banquet, because he, as he says, drinks water, his purpose being to sit up at night and compose speeches against us - though he brings up his son in such drunkenness that the latter is sober neither night nor day. Furthermore he undertook to make derogatory remarks about Antony's mouth, this man who has shown so great licentiousness and impurity throughout his entire life that he would not keep his hands off even his closest kin, but let out his wife for hire and deflowered his daughter.

These particulars I shall leave as they stand and return to the point where I started. That Antony against whom he has inveighed, seeing Caesar exalted over our government, caused him by granting what seemed personal favours to a friend not to put into effect any of the projects that he had in mind. Nothing so diverts persons from objects which they may attain without caring to secure them righteously, as for those who fear such results to appear to endure the former's conduct willingly. These persons in authority have no regard for their own consciousness of guilt, but if they think they have been detected, they are ashamed and afraid: thereafter they usually take what is said to them as flattery and believe the opposite, and any action which may result from the words as a plot, being suspicious in the midst of their shame. Antony knew this thoroughly, and first of all he selected the Lupercalia and that procession in order that Caesar in the relaxation of his spirit and the fun of the affair might be rebuked with immunity, and next he selected the Forum and the rostra that his patron might be shamed by the very places. And he fabricated the commands from the populace, in order that hearing them Caesar might reflect not on what Antony was saying at the time, but on what the Roman people would order a man to say. How could he have believed that this injunction had really been laid upon any one, when he knew that the people had not voted anything of the kind and did not hear them shouting out. But it was right for him to hear this in the Roman Forum, where we had often joined in many deliberations for freedom, and beside the rostra from which we had sent forth thousands and thousands of measures in behalf of the democracy, and at the festival of the Lupercalia, in order that he should remember Romulus, and from the mouth of the consul that he might call to mind the deeds of the early consuls, and in the name of the people, that he might ponder the fact that he was undertaking to be tyrant not over Africans or Gauls or Egyptians, but over very Romans. These words made him turn about; they humiliated him. And whereas if anyone else had offered him the diadem, he might have taken it, he was then stopped short by that speech and felt a shudder of alarm.

These, then, are the deeds of Antony: he did not uselessly break a leg, in order himself to escape, nor burn off a hand, in order to frighten Porsenna, but by his cleverness and consummate skill he put an end to the tyranny of Caesar better than any spear of Decius and better than the sword of Brutus. But you, Cicero, what did you effect in your consulship, not to mention wise and good things, that was not deserving of the greatest punishment? Did you not throw our city into uproar and party strife when it was quiet and harmonious, and fill the Forum and Capitol with slaves, among others, that you had called to your aid? Did you not ruin miserably Catiline, who was overanxious for office, but otherwise guilty of no violence? Did you not pitiably destroy Lentulus and his followers, who were not guilty, not tried, and not convicted, in spite of the fact that you are always and everywhere prating interminably about the laws and about the courts? If anyone should take these phrases from your speeches, there is nothing left. You censured Pompey because he conducted the trial of Milo contrary to legalised precedent: yet you afforded Lentulus no privilege great or small that is enjoined in these cases, but without a speech or trial you cast him into prison, a man respectable, aged, whose ancestors had given many great pledges that he would be friendly to his country, and who by reason of his age and his character had no power to do anything revolutionary. What trouble did he have that would have been cured by the change of condition? What blessing did he possess that would not certainly be jeopardised by rebellion? What arms had he collected, what allies had he equipped, that a man who had been consul and was praetor should be so pitilessly and impiously cast into a cell without being allowed to say a word of defence or hear a single charge, and die there like the basest criminals? For this is what this excellent Tullius most of all desired - that in the Tullianum, the place that bears his name, he might put to death the grandson of that Lentulus who once became the head of the senate. What would he have done if he had obtained authority to bear arms, seeing that he accomplished so many things of such a nature by his words alone? These are your brilliant achievements, these are your great exhibitions of generalship; and not only were you condemned for them by the rest, but you were so ready to vote against your own self in the matter that you fled before your trial came on. Yet what greater demonstration of your blood guilt could there be than that you came in danger of perishing at the hands of those very persons in whose behalf you pretended you had done this, that you were afraid of the very ones whom you said you had benefited by these acts, and that you did not wait to hear from them or say a word to them, you clever, you extraordinary man, you aider of other people, but secured your safety by flight as if from a battle? And you are so shameless that you have undertaken to write a history of these events that I have related, whereas you ought to have prayed that no other man even should give an account of any of them: then you might at least derive this advantage, that your doings should die with you and no memory of them be transmitted to posterity. Now, gentlemen, if you want to laugh, listen to his clever device. He set himself the task of writing a history of the entire existence of the city (for he pretends to be a sophist and poet and philosopher and orator and historian), and he began not from the founding of it, like the rest are similarly busied, but from his own consulship, so that he might proceed backwards, making that the beginning of his account, and the kingdom of Romulus the end.

Tell me, now, you who write such things and do such things, what the excellent man ought to say in popular address and do in action: for you are better at advising others about any matter whatsoever than at doing your own duty, and better at rebuking others than at reforming yourself. Yet how much better it were for you instead of reproaching Antony with cowardice to lay aside yourself that effeminacy both of spirit and of body, instead of bringing a charge of disloyalty against him to cease yourself from doing anything disloyal or playing the deserter, instead of accusing him of ingratitude to cease yourself from wronging your benefactors! For this, I must tell you, is one of his inherent defects, that he hates above all those who have done him any favour, and is always fawning upon somebody else but plotting against these persons. To leave aside other instances, he was pitied and preserved by Caesar and enrolled among the patricians, after which he killed him - no, not with his own hand (he is too cowardly and womanish), but by persuading and making ready others who should do it. The men themselves showed that I speak the truth in this. When they ran out into the Forum with their naked blades, they invoked him by name, saying 'Cicero!' repeatedly, as you all heard. His benefactor, Caesar, then, he slew, and as for Antony from whom he obtained personally safety and a priesthood when he was in danger of perishing at the hands of the soldiers in Brundusium, he repays him with this sort of thanks, by accusing him for deeds with which neither he himself nor anyone else ever found any fault and attacking him for conduct which he praises in others. Yet he sees this Caesar (that is, Octavian Caesar), who has not attained the age yet to hold office or have any part in politics and has not been chosen by you, sees him equipped with power and standing as the author of a war without our vote or orders, and not only has no blame to bestow, but pronounces laudations. So you perceive that he investigates neither what is just with reference to the laws nor what is useful with reference to the public weal, but simply manages everything to suit his own will, censuring in some what he extols in others, spreads false reports against you, and calumniates you gratuitously. For you will find that all of Antony's acts after Caesar's demise were ordered by you. To speak about the disposition of the funds and the examination of the letters I deem to be superfluous. Why so? Because first it would be the business of the one who inherited his property to look into the matter, and second, if there was any truth in the charge of malfeasance, it ought to have been stopped then on the moment. For none of the transactions was carried on underhandedly, Cicero, but they were all recorded on tablets, as you yourself affirm. If Antony committed his many wrongs so openly and shamelessly as you say, and plundered the whole of Crete on the pretext that in accord with Caesar's letters it had been left free after the governorship of Brutus, though the latter was later given charge of it by us, how could you have kept silent and how could anyone else have borne it? But these matters, as I said, I shall pass over; for the majority of them have not been mentioned individually, and Antony is not present, who could inform you exactly of what he has done in each instance. As to Macedonia and Gaul and the remaining provinces and legions, yours are the decrees, Conscript Fathers, according to which you assigned to the various governors their separate charges and delivered to Antony Gaul, together with the soldiers. This is known also to Cicero. He was there and helped vote for all of them just like you. Yet how much better it would have been for him then to speak in opposition, if any item of business was not going as it should, and to instruct you in these matters that are now brought forward, than to be silent at the time and allow you to make mistakes, and now nominally to censure Antony but really to accuse the senate!

Any sensible person could not assert, either, that Antony forced you to vote these measures. He himself had no band of soldiers so as to compel you to do anything contrary to your inclinations, and further the business was done for the good of the city. For since the legions had been sent ahead and united, there was fear that when they heard of Caesar's assassination they might revolt, put some inferior man at their head, and begin to wage war again: so it seemed good to you, taking a proper and excellent course, to place in command of them Antony the consul, who was charged with the promotion of harmony, who had rejected the dictatorship entirely from the system of government. And that is the reason that you gave him Gaul in place of Macedonia, that he should stay here in Italy, committing no harm, and do at once whatever errand was assigned him by you.

This I have said to you that you may know that you decided rightly. For Cicero that other point of mine was sufficient, namely, that he was present during all these proceedings and helped us to pass the measures, though Antony had not a soldier at the time and could not have brought to bear on us pressure in the shape of any terror that would have made us neglect a single point of our interest. But even if you were then silent, tell us now at least: what ought we to have done under the circumstances? Leave the legions leaderless? Would they have failed to fill both Macedonia and Italy with countless evils? Commit them to another? And whom could we have found more closely related and suited to the business than Antony, the consul, the director of all the city's affairs, the one who had taken such good care of harmony among us, the one who had given countless examples of his affection for the State? Some one of the assassins, perhaps? Why, it wasn't even safe for them to live in the city. Some one of the party opposed to them? Everybody suspected those people. What other man was there surpassing him in esteem, excelling him in experience? Or are you vexed that we did not choose you? What kind of administration would you have given? What would you not have done when you got arms and soldiers, considering that you occasioned so many and so great instances of turmoil in your consulship as a result of these elaborate antitheses, which you have made your specialty, of which alone you were master. But I return to my point that you were present when it was being voted and said nothing against it, but assented to all the measures as being obviously excellent and necessary. You did not lack opportunity to speak; indeed you roared out considerable that was beside the purpose. Nor were you afraid of anybody. How could you, who did not fear the armed warrior, have quailed before the defenceless man? Or how have feared him alone when you do not dread him in the possession of many soldiers! Yes, you also give yourself airs for absolutely despising death, as you affirm.

Since these facts are so, which of the two, senators, seems to be in the wrong, Antony, who is managing the forces granted him by us, or Caesar, who is surrounded with such a large band of his own? Antony, who has departed to take up the office committed to him by us, or Brutus, who prevents him from setting foot in the country? Antony, who wishes to compel our allies to obey our decrees, or they, who have not received the ruler sent them by us but have attached themselves to the man who was voted against? Antony, who keeps our soldiers together, or the soldiers, who have abandoned their commander? Antony, who has introduced not one of these soldiers granted him by us into the city, or Caesar, who by money persuaded those who had long ago been in service to come here? I think there is no further need of argument to answer the imputation that he does not seem to be managing correctly all the duties laid upon him by us, and to show that these men ought to suffer punishment for what they have ventured on their own responsibility. Therefore you also secured the guard of soldiers that you might discuss in safety the present situation, not on account of Antony, who had caused no trouble privately nor intimidated you in any way, but on account of his rival, who both had gathered a force against him and has often kept many soldiers in the city itself. I have said so much for Cicero's benefit, since it was he who began unfair argument against us. I am not generally quarrelsome, as he is, nor do I care to pry into others' misdeeds, as he continually gives himself airs for doing. Now I will tell you what advice I have to give, not favouring Antony at all nor calumniating Caesar or Brutus, but planning for the common advantage, as is proper. I declare that we ought not yet to make an enemy of either of these men in arms nor to enquire exactly what they have been doing or in what way. The present crisis is not suitable for this action, and as they are all alike our fellow-citizens, if any one of them fails the loss will be ours, or if any one of them succeeds his aggrandisement will be a menace to us. Wherefore I believe that we ought to treat them as friends and citizens and send messengers to all of them alike, bidding them lay down their arms and put themselves and their legions in our hands, and that we ought not yet to wage war on any one of them, but after their replies have come back approve those who are willing to obey us and fight against the disobedient. This course is just and expedient for us - not to be in a hurry or do anything rashly, but to wait and after giving the leaders themselves and their soldiers an opportunity to change their minds, then, if in such case there be need of war, to give the consuls charge of it.

And you, Cicero, I advise not to show a womanish sauciness, nor to imitate Bambalio even in making war, nor, because of your private enmity toward Antony, to plunge the whole city publicly again into danger. You will do well if you even become reconciled to him, with whom you have often enjoyed friendly intercourse. But even if you continue embittered against him, at least spare us, and do not after acting as the promoter of friendship among us then destroy it. Remember that day and the speech which you delivered in the precinct of Tellus, and yield a little to this goddess of Concord under whose guidance we are now deliberating, and avoid discrediting those statements and making them appear as if not uttered from a sincere heart, or by somebody else on that occasion. This is to the advantage of the State and will bring you most renown. Do not think that audacity is either glorious or safe, and do not feel sure of being praised just for saying that you despise death. Such men all suspect and hate as being likely to venture some deed of evil through desperation. Those whom they see, however, paying greatest attention to their own safety they praise and laud, because such would not willingly do anything that merited death. Do you, therefore, if you honestly wish your country to be safe, speak and act in such a way as will both preserve yourself and not, by Jupiter, involve us in your destruction!'

APPENDIX 4

Extract from The Wars of the Jews *by Flavius Josephus (AD 37-100), Book 1, Chapter 18*

But Herod's concern at present, now he had his enemies under his power, was to restrain the zeal of his foreign auxiliaries; for the multitude of the strange people were very eager to see the temple, and what was sacred in the holy house itself; but the king endeavoured to restrain them, partly by his exhortations, partly by his threatenings, nay, partly by force, as thinking the victory worse than a defeat to him, if any thing that ought not to be seen were seen by them. He also forbade, at the same time, the spoiling of the city, asking Sosius in the most earnest manner, whether the Romans, by thus emptying the city of money and men, had a mind to leave him king of a desert - and told him that he judged the dominion of the habitable earth too small a compensation for the slaughter of so many citizens. And when Sosius said that it was but just to allow the soldiers this plunder as a reward for what they suffered during the siege, Herod made answer, that he would give every one of the soldiers a reward out of his own money. So he purchased the deliverance of his country, and performed his promises to them, and made presents after a magnificent manner to each soldier, and proportionably to their commanders, and with a most royal bounty to Sosius himself, whereby nobody went away but in a wealthy condition. Hereupon Sosius dedicated a crown of gold to God, and then went away from Jerusalem, leading Antigonus away in bonds to Antony; then did the axe bring him to his end, who still had a fond desire of life, and some frigid hopes of it to the last, but by his cowardly behaviour well deserved to die by it.

Hereupon king Herod distinguished the multitude that was in the city; and for those that were of his side, he made them still more his friends by the honours he conferred on them; but for those of Antigonus' party, he slew them; and as his money ran low, he turned all the ornaments he had into money, and sent it to Antony, and to those about him. Yet could he not hereby purchase an exemption from all sufferings; for Antony was now bewitched by his love to Cleopatra, and was entirely conquered by her charms. Now Cleopatra had put to death all her kindred, till no one near her in blood remained alive, and after that she fell a slaying those no way related to her. So she calumniated the principal men among the Syrians to Antony, and persuaded him to have them slain, that so she might easily gain to be mistress of what they had; nay, she extended her avaricious humour to the Jews and Arabians, and secretly laboured to have

Herod and Malichus, the kings of both those nations, slain by his order.

Now is to these her injunctions to Antony, he complied in part; for though he esteemed it too abominable a thing to kill such good and great kings, yet was he thereby alienated from the friendship he had for them. He also took away a great deal of their country; nay, even the plantation of palm trees at Jericho, where also grows the balsam tree, and bestowed them upon her; as also all the cities on this side the river Eleutherus, Tyre and Sidon excepted. And when she was become mistress of these, and had conducted Antony in his expedition against the Parthians as far as Euphrates, she came by Apamia and Damascus into Judea and there did Herod pacify her indignation at him by large presents. He also hired of her those places that had been torn away from his kingdom, at the yearly rent of two hundred talents. He conducted her also as far as Pelusium, and paid her all the respects possible. Now it was not long after this that Antony was come back from Parthia, and led with him Artabazes, Tigranes's son, captive, as a present for Cleopatra; for this Parthian was presently given her, with his money, and all the prey that was taken with him.

which engines her purpose shook and gave way, so that she suffered those about her to give her what meat or medicine they pleased.

Some few days after, Caesar himself came to make her a visit and comfort her. She lay then upon her pallet-bed in undress, and, on his entering in, sprang up from off her bed, having nothing on but the one garment next her body, and flung herself at his feet, her hair and face looking wild and disfigured, her voice quivering, and her eyes sunk in her head. The marks of the blows she had given herself were visible about her bosom, and altogether her whole person seemed no less afflicted than her soul. But, for all this, her old charm, and the boldness of her youthful beauty had not wholly left her, and, in spite of her present condition, still sparkled from within, and let itself appear in all the movements of her countenance. Caesar, desiring her to repose herself, sat down by her; and, on this opportunity, she said something to justify her actions, attributing what she had done to the necessity she was under, and to her fear of Antony; and when Caesar, on each point, made his objections, and she found herself confuted, she broke off at once into language of entreaty and deprecation, as if she desired nothing more than to prolong her life. And at last, having by her a list of her treasure, she gave it into his hands; and when Seleucus, one of her stewards, who was by, pointed out that various articles were omitted, and charged her with secreting them, she flew up and caught him by the hair, and struck him several blows on the face. Caesar smiled and withheld her. 'Is it not very hard, Caesar,' said she, 'when you do me the honour to visit me in this condition I am in, that I should be accused by one of my own servants of laying by some women's toys, not meant to adorn, to be sure, my unhappy self, but that I might have some little present by me to make your Octavia and your Livia, that by their intercession I might hope to find you in some measure disposed to mercy?' Caesar was pleased to hear her talk thus, being now assured that she was desirous to live. And, therefore, letting her know that the things she had laid by she might dispose of as she pleased, and his usage of her should be honourable above her expectation, he went away, well satisfied that he had overreached her, but, in fact, was himself deceived.

There was a young man of distinction among Caesar's companions, named Cornelius Dolabella. He was not without a certain tenderness for Cleopatra, and sent her word privately, as she had besought him to do, that Caesar was about to return through Syria, and that she and her children were to be sent on within three days. When she understood this, she made her request to Caesar that he would be pleased to permit her to make oblations to the departed Antony; which being granted, she ordered herself to be carried to the place where he was buried, and there, accompanied by her women, she embraced his tomb with tears in her eyes, and spoke in this manner: 'O, dearest Antony,' said she, 'it is not long since that with these hands I buried you; then they were free, now I am a captive, and pay these last duties to you with a guard upon me, for fear that my just griefs and sorrows should impair my servile body, and make it less fit to appear in their triumph over you. No further offerings or libations expect from me; these are the last honours that Cleopatra can pay your memory, for she is to be hurried away far from you. Nothing could part us whilst we lived, but death seems to threaten to divide us. You, a Roman born, have found a grave in Egypt; I, an Egyptian, am to seek that favour, and none but that, in your country. But if the gods below, with whom you now are, either can or will do anything (since those above have betrayed us), suffer not your living wife to be abandoned; let me not be led in triumph to your shame, but hide me and bury me here with you, since, amongst all my bitter misfortunes, nothing has afflicted me like this brief time that I have lived away from you.'

Having made these lamentations, crowning the tomb with garlands and kissing it, she gave orders to prepare her a bath, and, coming out of the bath, she lay down and made a sumptuous meal. And a country fellow brought her a little basket, which the guards intercepting and asking what it was, the fellow put the leaves which lay uppermost aside, and showed them it was full of figs; and on their admiring the largeness and beauty of the figs, he laughed, and invited them to take some, which they refused, and, suspecting nothing, bade him carry them in. After her repast, Cleopatra sent to Caesar a letter which she had written and sealed; and, putting everybody out of the monument but her two women, she shut the doors. Caesar, opening her letter, and finding pathetic prayers and entreaties that she might be buried in the same tomb with Antony, soon guessed what she was doing. At first he was going himself in all haste, but, changing his mind, he sent others to see. The thing had been quickly done. The messengers came at full speed, and found the guards apprehensive of nothing; but on opening the doors, they saw her stone dead, lying upon a bed of gold, set out in all her royal ornaments. Iras, one of her women, lay dying at her feet, and Charmion, just ready to fall, scarce able to hold up her head, was adjusting her mistress's diadem. And when one that came in said angrily, 'Was this well done of your lady, Charmion?' 'Extremely well,' she answered, 'and as became the descendant of so many kings'; and as she said this, she fell down dead by the bedside.

Some relate that an asp was brought in amongst those figs and covered with the leaves, and that Cleopatra had arranged that it might settle on her before she knew, but, when she took away some of the figs and saw it, she said, 'So here it is,' and held out her bare arm to be bitten. Others say that it was kept in a vase, and that she vexed and pricked it with a golden spindle till it seized her arm. But what really took place is known to no one. Since it was also said that she carried poison in a hollow bodkin, about which she wound her hair; yet there was not so much as a spot found, or any symptom of poison upon her body, nor was the asp seen within the monument; only something like the trail of it was said to have been noticed on the sand by the sea, on the part towards which the building faced and where the windows were. Some relate that two faint puncture-marks were found on Cleopatra's arm, and to this account Caesar seems to have given credence; for in his triumph there was carried a figure of Cleopatra, with an asp clinging to her. Such are the various accounts. But Caesar, though much disappointed by her death, yet could not but admire the greatness of her spirit, and gave order that her body should he buried by Antony with royal splendour and magnificence. Her women, also, received honourable burial by his directions. Cleopatra had lived nine and thirty years, during twenty-two of which she had reigned as queen, and for fourteen had been Antony's partner in his empire. Antony, according to some authorities, was fifty-three, according to others, fifty-six years old. His statues were all thrown down, but those of Cleopatra were left untouched; for Archibius, one of her friends, gave Caesar two thousand talents to save them from the fate of Antony's.

Antony left by his three wives seven children, of whom only Antyllus, the eldest, was put to death by Caesar; Octavia took the rest, and brought them up with her own. Cleopatra, his daughter by Cleopatra, was given in marriage to Juba, the most accomplished of kings; and Antony, his son by Fulvia, attained such high favour, that whereas Agrippa was considered to hold the first place with Caesar, and the sons of Livia the second, the third, without dispute, was possessed by Antony. Octavia, also, having had by her first husband, Marcellus, two daughters, and one son named Marcellus, this son Caesar adopted, and gave him his daughter in marriage; as did Octavia one of the daughters to Agrippa. But Marcellus dying almost immediately after his marriage, she, perceiving that her brother was at a loss to find elsewhere any sure friend to be his son-in-law, was the first to recommend that Agrippa should put away her daughter and marry Julia. To this Caesar first, and then Agrippa himself, gave assent; so Agrippa married Julia, and Octavia, receiving her daughter, married her to the young Antony. Of the two daughters whom Octavia had borne to Antony, the one was married to Domitius Ahenobarbus; and the other, Antonia, famous for her beauty and discretion, was married to Drusus, the son of Livia, and step-son to Caesar. Of these parents were born Germanicus and Claudius. Claudius reigned later; and of the children of Germanicus, Caius, after a reign of distinction, was killed with his wife and child; Agrippina, after bearing a son, Lucius Domitius, to Ahenobarbus, was married to Claudius Caesar, who adopted Domitius, giving him the name of Nero Germanicus. He was emperor in our time, and put his mother to death, and with his madness and folly came not far from ruining the Roman empire, being Antony's descendant in the fifth generation.

APPENDIX 6

DEITIES OF ANCIENT EGYPT, GREECE AND ROME

Ancient Egypt

Many of the deities of ancient Egypt are known today by their Greek names due to the fact that they have been passed down to modern times in the language of ancient Greece. The ancient Egyptian versions only became known after hieroglyphs were deciphered in the nineteenth century.

AMUN (in Greek, AMMON)

Amun, whose name means 'Hidden' or 'Invisible one', had his origins as an obscure god of the air, and of fertility. He rose to prominence in the Twelfth Dynasty (1963-1786 BC) thanks to the patronage of the kings of the time; and in the Eighteenth Dynasty (1550-1295 BC) he became state god of Egypt. His chief centre of worship was the great temple of Karnak in the town known today as Luxor. The ancient Egyptians knew Luxor as 'The City of Amun' or just 'The City'. Homer called it Thebes, possibly as a compliment to his own Greek city of that name. Like other Egyptian gods, Amun had an animal that was associated with him, a relic of the time when Egyptians worshipped animal deities. Amun's sacred animal was a ram, identified with the males of a local breed of sheep that were famed for their particularly large, down-curved horns, and, like Amun himself, for their virility. Amun was never depicted in the shape of a ram but always in human form, wearing a cap surmounted by two tall plumes and a sun's disk. The mysterious, hidden part of his nature implicit in his name was expressed by the custom of covering the shrine in which the statue of the god was kept with a veil. His power remained undiminished for centuries: the Greeks worshipped him under the name Zeus-Ammon, the Romans under the name Jupiter-Ammon. His lasting importance was demonstrated by Alexander the Great's visit to his Oracle in the Siwa Oasis (see page 22); and by the fact that Alexander was represented, on coins especially, wearing the distinctive ram's horns of Amun. It is because of their resemblance to these horns that the fossils of certain marine cephalopods are known today as ammonites

EDJO see **WADJET**

HATHOR
Hathor had her cult centre at Denderah, on the left bank of the Nile some 60 km (37 miles) north of Luxor. She was worshipped there from very early times but the large,

well-preserved temple that stands there today was begun in the reigns of the later Ptolemies and completed in Roman times. Caesar Augustus (Octavian) allowed himself to be represented on its walls and ordered the construction of several subsidiary buildings, notably a small temple dedicated to Isis (the Iseum) which, ironically, stands within a few metres of the rear wall of the main temple which is decorated with reliefs showing his vanquished enemy, Cleopatra, with her son by Julius Caesar, Caesarion. Hathor was worshipped at many other places in Egypt. Her sacred animal was a cow. From very early times, cow goddesses were venerated by ancient Egyptians, as might be expected in an agricultural society: to them, a cow was the embodiment of fertility. Hathor was not only a symbol of fecundity but was also regarded as a sky goddess, the personification of the sky itself. Hence, her name, *Hwt-Hor*, means 'The Mansion of Horus', reference to the fact that she was believed to be the sky in which the sacred falcon (see under Horus) flew. The Egyptians visualised her as a gigantic cow which straddled the earth, her feet planted at the four cardinal points: her belly was the sky, her udders and the pattern on her hide were the planets and the stars. Between her horns she carried a sundisk, and she was regarded as the Eye of the Sun God, Re (see below). Artistic representations depict her either as an actual cow, or as a woman with a cow's head, or as a woman wearing upon her head a sundisk set between a pair of cow's horns. Horus (see below) was her husband; their sons were *Hor-sma-tawy* - rendered in Greek as Harsomtus - whose name means 'Horus-who-unites-the-Two-Lands' (Egypt); and Ihy, the musician god. Harsomtus was born as the result of the divine marriage between Hathor and Horus (see below), which was celebrated annually when the cult statue of the goddess was taken out of her temple and conveyed south along the Nile to the temple of her husband at Edfu (see below) during the third month of summer (May) on the night of the new moon. The Greeks identified Hathor with their own goddess of love and beauty, Aphrodite (see below). For the Egyptians she was their Golden One, the joyous goddess of love, music and intoxication, the bringer of happiness.

HORUS

Horus was one of many falcon gods in ancient Egypt: there were even several different falcon gods called Horus. The most famous of these, however, was Horus of Edfu. In reliefs on temple walls he is usually depicted as a falcon-headed man; his cult statues are always in the form of a falcon. Originally, Horus was a sky god but his greatest claim to fame was as the son of Isis (see below) and Osiris (see below). He was born posthumously after his father, Osiris, was killed by his brother, Seth. When Horus was fifteen years old, he claimed the throne of Egypt that his murdered father had once occupied. Seth challenged his nephew's right to the throne and it was only after eighty years of struggle that Horus managed to vanquish him. He cut off Seth's head and dragged his body the length and breadth of Egypt with spears stuck into its back. Horus became the mythological King of Egypt. In real life, each reigning King of Egypt was regarded as the living Horus, the embodiment of the god. One of the names in the royal titulary, the Horus Name, was symbolic of the king's role as Horus incarnate. His huge temple at Edfu, on the west bank of the Nile some 100 km (62 miles) south of Luxor, on the site of a much older temple, also dedicated to Horus, was begun in 237 BC in the reign of Ptolemy III Euergetes I, and finished in 57 BC. It was the only Ptolemaic temple to be completed, and today is in an almost complete state of preservation and is regarded as one of the most important religious monuments in Egypt.

ISIS

Isis was one of four siblings born to the great sun god, Re (see below). Her brother, Seth, was married to their sister, Nephthys; and she herself was married to their brother, Osiris (see below). She was famed as the greatest magician of all, having duped her father, Re, himself noted for his magical abilities, out of his secrets. After her husband's murder, Isis set out on a quest to find his body, which his murderer, Seth, had dismembered and scattered all over Egypt. She succeeded in finding all the parts with the exception of his penis, which had been thrown into the Nile, where it was swallowed by a Mormyrus, or Oxyrhynchus, fish (elephant-snout fish). Isis reassembled her husband's body, then changed herself into a kite and used her wings to fan air into it, bringing Osiris back to life. He was unable to take his place on earth again but took up residence in the world of the dead, there to reign as king. In spite of the fact that Osiris had lost his penis, Isis - the great magician - managed to make herself pregnant with his son, Horus. She then sought refuge in the marshes of the Nile Delta until Horus was of an age to challenge his uncle Seth for the right to rule Egypt and to seek vengeance for his father's death. Isis typified the wife, faithful to her husband even after death, and the mother, devoted to her child. Her fame as a magician, in particular her perceived willingness to use her magic powers to care for children, made her the most popular goddess in the Egyptian pantheon. Her cult spread throughout the ancient world; and in the first century BC she was the most popular goddess in Rome. As mentioned earlier, the cult of Isis was superseded only by that of the Virgin Mary; and the iconography of Mary with the Christ Child seated upon her knee was derived from that of Isis, who was often depicted suckling her son, Horus. The most famous temple dedicated to Isis lies on the island of Philae on the southern border of Egypt, largely built in the reigns of Ptolemaic kings and Roman and Byzantine Emperors.

MAAT

Maat, the daughter of Re (see below), was the personification of Truth and Justice. In artistic representations she is depicted as a woman wearing an ostrich plume on her head. This feather was used in hieroglyphic writing to represent not only Maat's name but also the noun 'truth'. Scenes painted upon the walls of tombs showing the Judgement of the Dead depict the deceased person's heart being weighed in a balance again the feather of Maat to gauge whether he has lived according to maat, that is, had lived in conformity with truth and justice.

NEKHBET

Nekhbet (She-of-Nekheb) was the local goddess of the city of Nekheb, which lies on the east bank of the Nile some 80 km (50 miles) south of Luxor. She was originally worshipped in the form of *Vultur auricularis*, the Sociable Vulture, and from the earliest times was regarded as the principal goddess of Upper, or southern, Egypt, whose counterpart in Lower (northern) Egypt was the cobra goddess, Wadjet (see below). They were known as the Two Ladies, or *nebty*, and the first king of Egypt, Menes, chose them to symbolise his unification of the two halves of Egypt into one kingdom by adopting a title known as the *nebty*-name. In hieroglyphic script, the nebty-name is written showing a vulture and a cobra sitting in a basket; and the name formed part of the titulary of the king of Egypt. Nekhbet was particularly concerned with the crown of Upper Egypt, the White Crown, and with the protection of its wearer. She and her counterpart, Wadjet, formed part of the royal diadem known as the uraeus (see page 130).

OSIRIS

Osiris is perhaps the most famous and popular of the gods of ancient Egypt, worshipped all over Egypt and beyond but whose principal cult centre was at Abydos, which lies on the edge of the western desert near the modern town of el-Baliana. He was a god whose story appealed to his worshippers because of its humanity - a king betrayed and brutally murdered but restored to life through the devotion of his wife, Isis (see above). His story tells of how his wife sought out the scattered pieces of his body, and as she found each piece ordered a temple to be erected on the site. Such was the desire of the ancient Egyptians to honour Osiris that his temples proliferated, each one claiming to be founded in the place where a piece of his body was buried. The priesthood of his Memphis temple, for example, claimed that his head was buried there; but the same claim was made at Abydos. Through his resurrection, Osiris held out the hope of eternal life, at first to the king of Egypt alone but eventually to every Egyptian. Wrapped in bandages in imitation of those in which Osiris' body had been wrapped, every dead Egyptian who could afford a burial was identified with Osiris and addressed as 'the Osiris', which in effect meant deceased. Osiris was king of the Afterlife, the great judge of the dead; and thanks to his resurrection, a potent symbol of fertility. Representations of Osiris show him shrouded in a tight-fitting white garment, which indicated mummy-bandages, his arms protruding from the garment and holding the crook and the flail, symbols of kingship. On his head he wears a tall crown flanked by two plumes. Other deities often look alike, with only their names written in hieroglyphs to identify them. Osiris is unmistakable.

RE

Re was thought to be the self-engendered eternal spirit who first appeared on earth floating on the primordial waters that covered it, seated upon a giant blue lotus, a *Nymphaea cerulea*, whose beautiful perfume suggested to the Egyptians the scent of Re's divine sweat. From his sweat, Re was said to have created the gods; from his tears he created mankind. Re's chief centre of worship was at Iunu, known to the Greeks as Heliopolis or City of the Sun, for Re was a sun god, envisioned as the disk of the sun at midday. In his prime he ruled mankind as King of Egypt, but as he grew old his grip on the throne weakened. He was tricked by Isis into revealing the Secret Name under which he exerted great magical powers; and mankind grew so rebellious that he decided to send Hathor to destroy them. He relented and retired. He made himself responsible for the Afterlife, and became the Great Judge of the Dead. By day he sailed across the sky in his celestial boat, by night he sailed through the Underworld. Kings of Egypt were closely associated with him: two of the names in the royal titulary, 'Son of Re' and 'King of Upper and Lower Egypt' were written inside cartouches; the ancient Egypt term for cartouche was *shen*, which means 'that which the sun's disk encircles'. It was intended to show that the king ruled the world, a world that was illuminated by Re.

SERAPIS

The god introduced into Egypt by Ptolemy I Soter in an attempt to provide all his subjects, both Greek and Egyptian, with a deity that they would find sympathetic. Serapis was a combination of Osiris and Apis, the sacred bull that was worshipped in Memphis, but with many Hellenistic elements also. He took some of his attributes from Zeus, Dionysus and Asklepios, god of healing and medicine. Thus Serapis was a physician and a god of fertility. His cult was centred on Alexandria, where his temple, the Serapeum, became a place of pilgrimage for Greeks and Romans until its destruction in AD 389 on the orders of the Emperor Theodosius. The Egyptians never fully accepted this hybrid deity with his Hellenistic overtones.

WADJET

The goddess Wadjet is often known by her Greek name, Edjo. Her chief cult centre was Dep, a town in the north-western Nile Delta, where she was worshipped as a cobra. She was closely associated with the crown of Lower Egypt, the Red Crown. She and her counterpart, Nekhbet (see above) attended the coronation of a king. Although both goddesses are usually shown in the form of a vulture (Nekhbet) and a cobra (Wadjet), in temple reliefs depicting a coronation, they are shown in human female form, with Nekhbet crowning the king with the White Crown of Upper Egypt and Wadjet crowning him with the Red Crown of Lower Egypt.

Greece and Rome
APHRODITE, known to the Romans as Venus

Aphrodite was the goddess of beauty, love and fertility. She was said to have been born near Cythera, from sea-foam, Greek *aphros*, from whence her name was derived. She went to Cyprus and there a sanctuary was built for her at Paphos. Homer claimed that she was the daughter of Zeus. Her husband was Hephaistos, son of Zeus and Hera, the lame god of fire and forge. When Hephaistos discovered that his wife was being unfaithful to him with Ares, he made a net of gold which he hung over Aphrodite's bed; and in the middle of their love-making, he cut its supports so that it fell over the lovers, entangling them. He then summoned the gods to witness Aphrodite's infidelity, humiliating her. She later fell in love with Adonis, a beautiful youth; and she was also associated with Eros (Roman Cupid), the mischievous god of love and sexual attraction. She seduced Anchises, a minor member of the ruling house of Troy, and became the mother of Aeneas, the Trojan hero who survived the war and went on to Italy where he became the ancestral hero of the Romans.

APOLLO

Apollo is often said to be the 'most Greek of all gods'. He and his sister, Artemis, were the twin children of Zeus and the Titan goddess, Leto. When Hera discovered that Leto was pregnant, she was jealous and sent the Python, the great serpent that guarded the omphalos (navel), the stone that marked the centre of the earth, to harry her ceaselessly so that she could never lie down to give birth wherever the sun shone. Zeus took pity on her and sent the north wind, the Boreas, to convey her to safety, which she found on the small, rocky island of Delos, where she gave birth to her twins. When Apollo grew up, he determined to avenge his mother by killing the Python. He made his way to the slopes of Mount Parnassus where the serpent lived and found it at the Oracle of Gaia, the earth goddess, in Delphi. There, Apollo entered the sacred precinct and slew the Python with his arrows. He took over the Oracle, which, presided over by a priestess called the Pythia, became the most famous and revered of all the Oracles in the Greek and Roman world. The Pythia was consulted on major matters such as the likely outcome of a war, she was also consulted on more personal affairs such a whether a man should marry - the replies were typically ambiguous. Apollo was not only an avenging archer, he had a more serene side to his nature as the patron of music, medicine and philosophy. In sculpture he was the ideal of young male beauty; and in the Hellenistic period became identified with the Sun. The Romans called him Phoebus (bright) Apollo.

ARES, known to the Romans as Mars

Ares was the son of Zeus and Hera. He was the god of war and fighting, and although his cult was important in Greek Thebes, elsewhere he was regarded as an unpopular and relatively minor deity, often treated with contempt and revulsion in Greek literature because of his destructive and destabilising nature.

ARTEMIS, known to the Romans as Diana

Artemis was known to the Greeks as the twin sister of Apollo. She was the first to be born and helped her mother deliver her twin, which led to her taking a particular interest in the young of animals, including human animals. Greek women prayed to her for protection in childbirth. She was idealised as a virgin huntress, having asked her father, Zeus, to allow her never to marry. The myth of Artemis and Actaeon tells of how her hunting companion, Actaeon, came upon her naked bathing a spring and tried to rape her. As a punishment, Artemis turned him into a stag, whereupon his hounds tore him to pieces. Another myth concerns Orion, the favourite hunting companion of the goddess and one whom she loved. After she accidentally shot an arrow into him and killed him, Zeus set him among the stars as the constellation Orion. Another version of his death relates that he was stung and killed by a giant scorpion, which has given its name to the constellation, Scorpio. Artemis was an ancient mother-goddess who was associated with woods and hills: her famous cult at Ephesus owed its origins to her identification with an ancient Anatolian mother-goddess.

DIANA see Artemis

DIONYSUS, known to the Romans as Bacchus

Dionysus was the son of Zeus and a mortal woman, Semele, who was a princess of Thracian-Phrygian origin. Zeus seduced Semele and made her pregnant, whereupon a jealous Hera convinced her husband's lover that she should persuade Zeus to reveal himself in all his terrible glory to prove his love for her. A reluctant Zeus did so, aware that no human being could look upon him and survive. Semele was consumed by flames, but Zeus retrieved the child within her and sewed him into his thigh until it was time for him to be born. Dionysus was thus often called 'the twice born'. He was a complex deity, worshipped at Delphi and in some mystery cults as a child-god. He was the god of wine and of vegetation. In the earliest form of his cult, his devotees, mainly women, danced in drunken frenzies at night in the mountains to the music of flutes and drums. They tore animals apart and ate the pieces raw: they were prepared to do the same to human beings who threatened Dionysus, as King Pentheus of Thebes found to his cost. The Greeks 'civilized' Dionysus and he became the patron of drama and the theatre.

JUPITER see Zeus

MARS

In ancient Roman religion and myth, Mars was the god of war. He was second in importance only to Jupiter and, naturally, was especially venerated by the Roman army. In the Roman calendar, March, in Latin Martius, was the month named in his honour. Mars was identified with the Greek god, Ares, but he was considered to be a much more dignified character than Ares. Mars represented military power as a way to secure peace. His liaison with the goddess Venus led to the birth of the Trojan hero, Aeneas. Rhea Silvia, a Vestal Virgin and as such sworn to celibacy, became pregnant and claimed that Mars had raped her. She gave birth to twins, Romulus and Remus, and was buried alive for her transgression. An order was given that the twins be put to death. However, the servant who was charged with the task took pity on them and placed them in a basket which he set adrift on the river Tiber. The twins were rescued by a she-wolf who suckled them until they were weaned. In due course they went on to found Rome; and Mars, their father, became the divine father of all Romans. The large, publicly owned area of Rome was named Campus Martius (field of Mars). His cult-centre was located outwith the boundaries of the City, but Caesar Augustus made Mars the focus of Roman religion by establishing a temple for him within the Forum, the great public space that was the centre for economic and judicial business.

NEMESIS

Nemesis was the goddess of retribution against those who succumb to hubris (arrogance before the gods). There was no escape from her, hence she was sometimes called Adrasteia or Adrestia, meaning 'the inescapable'.

VENUS see Aphrodite

ZEUS, known to the Romans as Jupiter

Zeus was the son of Kronos, one of the Titans, known as the Elder Gods, who ruled the Cosmos before the deities of Olympus came into being. Having deposed and castrated his father, Ouranos (Uranus, the Sky), Kronos became king of Time but lived in fear lest he in his turn would be overthrown by a son born to him. Accordingly, he swallowed every child born to him by his wife, Rhea. Rhea managed to save her youngest son, Zeus, by hiding him in a cave in Crete after she had duped Kronos into thinking he had swallowed the child by feeding him a stone wrapped in swaddling clothes. When Zeus came of age, he deposed his father and forced him to disgorge the children he had swallowed, after which he led his brothers and sisters to Mount Olympus, which became the dwelling place of the twelve Olympian gods - Zeus, Hera, Poseidon, Athena, Apollo, Artemis, Hestia, Demeter, Hermes, Aphrodite, Ares and Hephaestus. The Olympian gods defeated the Titans in a great battle, and drove them down into the pit known as Tartarus, the most dreadful place in the Underworld, although aeons later Zeus released Kronos and the other Titans and made Kronos ruler of the Elysian Fields, home of the blessed dead. Mount Olympus was where the throne of the king of the gods, Zeus, was located, and was the place from which the Olympian gods decided the fate of mankind. In origin, Zeus was a sky god: he was known as cloud-gatherer, rain-giver and thunderer, and so naturally was associated with mountains. He was regarded as the protector of kings and cities and as the custodian of law and morality. He was the Father of Gods and Men, not as their creator but as their overlord.

NOTES

Chapter 1

1 The scholar-priest, Manetho, who lived during the reign of Ptolemy I, divided Egyptian history into thirty dynasties, or ruling houses, ending with the death of the last native Egyptian ruler, Nectanebo II, in 343 BC. In modern times, two further dynasties are often appended to Manetho's original list - the 31st or Persian, and the 32nd or Ptolemaic.

2 The following love poem illustrates the ancient Egyptian ideal of feminine beauty:

Of surpassing radiance and luminous skin,
With lovely, clear-gazing eyes,
Her lips speak sweetly
With not a word too much,
Her neck is long, her breast is white,
Her hair is veritable lapis lazuli.
Her arm surpasses gold
And her fingers are like lotus buds.

With rounded thighs and trim waist,
Her legs display her beauty when,
With graceful gait she treads the earth.

Author's translation from the first stanza in Papyrus Chester
Beatty I.

Chapter 2

1 Strabo, *Geographia* XVII, paragraph 8
2 The tomb of Alexander has not been found in modern
   times. The coastline has shifted so that it probably lies
   under the waters of the Bay of Alexandria. In the past few
   years extensive underwater excavations have been carried
   out, so who knows it may one day be discovered. Arab
   tradition has it that the Sema lies under the Mosque of
   Nebi Daniel in the centre of Alexandria.
3 The royal titulary consisted of five 'great names': 1. the Horus
   name, which represents the king as the earthly embodiment
   of the ancient falcon-god; 2. the Two Ladies name, the two
   ladies being Nekhbet and Edjo, divine guardians of the
   king; 3. the Golden Horus name; 4. the prenomen, which
   essentially means 'king of Upper and Lower Egypt' and
   which is normally written inside a cartouche; 5. the nomen,
   which is prefaced by the epithet 'son of (the sun god) Re'.
4 Elgood, 1938, p.vii
5 The word pharaoh is derived from the ancient Egyptian
   pr, meaning house, and *aa* meaning great. The 'Great
   House' was the royal palace: from about 1360 BC the
   term was used to refer to the inhabitant of the palace, that
   is, the king. The t in pr-aat feminises the term.

6 An apocryphal quote from the advice that Queen Victoria was supposed to have given one of her daughters on her wedding night.

Chapter 3
1 Appian, *The Civil Wars*, Book ii.
2 *Julius Caesar*, Act 1, Scene 2, lines 141-2.
3 *ibid.* Act 1, Scene 2, line 200.
4 *ibid.* Act 3, Scene 2, lines 70 foll.

Chapter 4
1 *Antony and Cleopatra*, Act 2, Scene 2, line 6 foll.
2 'It is never difficult to distinguish between a Scotsman with a grievance and a ray of sunshine'; P.G. Wodehouse, *Blandings Castle*, 1935.
3 *Macbeth*, Act 2, Scene 2, lines 62-3.
4 'Uraeus', the Latinised version of the Greek *ouraios*, meaning snake, the term applied to the royal diadem bearing a figure of the cobra-goddess, Wadjet, at the front.

Chapter 5
1 Chaucer, The Legend of Good Women, Prologue, Cleopatra, 1, 34.
2 *Antony and Cleopatra*, Act 1, Scene 1, line 12.
3 *ibid.* Act 5, Scene 2, lines 9-10.
4 W. Hazlitt, *The Plain Speaker: On the Pleasure of Hating*, Oxford, 1826, page 22.
5 *Antony and Cleopatra*, Act 1, Scene 3, line 68.
6 *ibid.* Act 5, Scene 2, line 356.

BIBLIOGRAPHY

BEVAN, E. R., *The House of Ptolemy*, Chicago, 1927.

BOWMAN, A. K., *Egypt after the Pharaohs*, London, 1986.

BRADFORD, E., *Cleopatra*, London, 1986.

CHAUCER, G., *The Complete Works*, London, 1912.

DRYDEN, J., *All for Love, or the World Well Lost*, 1677/1678

ELGOOD, P. G., *The Ptolemies of Egypt*, Bristol, 1938.

FORSTER, E. M., *Alexandria*, New York, 1961.

GODDIO, F. and MASSON-BERGHOFF, A., *Sunken Cities: Egypt's lost worlds*, London, 2016.

GRANT, M., *Cleopatra*, London, 1972.

HALLETT, L. H, *Cleopatra: Histories, Dreams and Distortions*, London, 1990.

HERODOTUS, *The Histories*, Harmondsworth, 1977.

MANNING, J. G., *The Last Pharaohs - Egypt under the Ptolemies 305-30*, Princeton, 2010.

MASSIE, A., *The Caesars*, London, 1983.

PLUTARCH, *Life of Antony*, Loeb Classical Library, 1920.

PLUTARCH, *Life of Pompey*, Loeb Classical Library, 1917.

RUGGIERO, P. de, *Mark Antony: A Plain, Blunt Man*, Barnsley, 2013.

SCHIFF, S., *Cleopatra: A Life*, London, 2010.

SHAKESPEARE, W., *Complete Works*, The Royal Shakespeare Company, 2007.

SOUTHERN, P., *Antony & Cleopatra*, Stroud, 2008.

SOUTHERN, P., *Mark Antony*, Stroud, 1998.

TYLDESLEY, J., *Cleopatra, Last Queen of Egypt*, London, 2008.

WEIGALL, A., *The Life and Times of Cleopatra, Queen of Egypt*, London, 1923.

INDEX